EMOTIONAL INTELLIGENCE

The Genius Guide to Maximizing Your Emotional Intelligence

(A Bold Recovery Guide to Save Your Anxious Mind From Addiction)

Rudolph Lemke

Published by Bengion Cosalas

Rudolph Lemke

All Rights Reserved

Emotional Intelligence: The Genius Guide to Maximizing Your Emotional Intelligence (A Bold Recovery Guide to Save Your Anxious Mind From Addiction)

ISBN 978-1-77485-279-8

All rights reserved. No part of this guide may be reproduced in any form without permission in writing from the publisher except in the case of brief quotations embodied in critical articles or reviews.

Legal & Disclaimer

The information contained in this book is not designed to replace or take the place of any form of medicine or professional medical advice. The information in this book has been provided for educational and entertainment purposes only.

The information contained in this book has been compiled from sources deemed reliable, and it is accurate to the best of the Author's knowledge; however, the Author cannot guarantee its accuracy and validity and cannot be held liable for any errors or omissions. Changes are periodically made to this book. You must consult your doctor or get professional medical advice before using any of the suggested remedies, techniques, or information in this book.

Upon using the information contained in this book, you agree to hold harmless the Author from and against any damages, costs, and expenses, including any legal fees potentially resulting from the application of any of the information provided by this guide. This disclaimer applies to any damages or injury caused by the use and application, whether directly or indirectly, of any advice or information presented, whether for breach of contract, tort, negligence, personal injury, criminal intent, or under any other cause of action.

You agree to accept all risks of using the information presented inside this book. You need to consult a professional medical practitioner in order to ensure you are both able and healthy enough to participate in this program.

Table of Contents

INTRODUCTION 1

CHAPTER 1: WHAT IS EMOTIONAL INTELLIGENCE (EQ) IS MADE OF? 2

CHAPTER 2: BEING IN CONTACT WITH YOUR FEELINGS 9

CHAPTER 3: RISE ABOVE THE HERD 25

CHAPTER 4: RELATING EMOTIONS.................................... 47

CHAPTER 5: THE ART OF SELF-CONFIDENCE..................... 54

CHAPTER 6: EQ VERSUS IQ 60

CHAPTER 7: THE EMOTIONAL HEALTH CHILDREN 74

CHAPTER 8: MOVING TOWARD THE POSITIVE 78

CHAPTER 9: WHAT IS EMOTIONAL INTELLIGENCE? 90

CHAPTER 10: TEACH YOUR CHILDREN TO RECOGNIZE THEIR EMOTIONAL INTELLIGENCE 104

CHAPTER 11: WORKING ON EMOTIONAL INTELLIGENCE 112

CHAPTER 12: FEELINGS ARE AN ANSWER TO YOUR INTERPRETATION OF INFORMATION . INTERPRETATIONS CAN BE ALTERED 118

CHAPTER 13: TRIGGERS OF EMOTION 127

CHAPTER 14: IDENTIFYING YOUR EMOTIONS AND THE EMOTIONS OF OTHERS... 131

CHAPTER 15: BUILDING ON SELF-CONFIDENCE.............. 146

CHAPTER 16: STRATEGIES TO INSPIRE INTEREST............ 157

CHAPTER 17: CONTROLLING YOUR THOUGHTS 163

CHAPTER 18: TRYING TO EMBRACE CRITICISM.............. 168

CHAPTER 19: LOOKING AT THINGS THROUGH A DETACHED EYE 175

CONCLUSION.. 184

Introduction

This book provides the most effective steps and strategies on how to get like them , who aren't only emotionally intelligent, but are generally more intelligent than everyone else.

People who are emotionally intelligent are the most ideal role models that you could find if you are also looking at being as similar to them. They aren't unlike you or other people. The thing that makes them different is their lifestyles. The various habits of the aforementioned are described in this book.

Chapter 1: What Is Emotional Intelligence (Eq) is Made Of?

The precise configurations of the EI cannot always be reached upon as it is extremely complex and complex. The fundamental concept is fairly simple to comprehend. Emotional Intelligence is the Emotional Intelligence is a measurement of capabilities, just like an Intelligence Quotient (IQ). But, unlike IQ which tends to be steady from the end of teens onwards Your EI is likely to grow and grow.

It is possible to begin improving this by becoming conscious of your self-awareness , and taking note of your thinking patterns and your feelings.

Emotional intelligence is mostly centered in the emotional portion that is the part of our brain more than the rational part of the brain. It's the degree of self-awareness and managing themselves (personal competency and interpersonal abilities) and their interpersonal awareness and relationship management (social ability and interpersonal abilities). All of these aspects are equally important and are interconnected. The emotional intelligence is connected to the rational portion of the brain in as the sense that those with higher levels of EI make use of their emotions to improve their ways of thinking and problem-solving. If you are aware of and are aware of your own emotions, you become self-aware and have clarity and a better understanding of your feelings.

If you're a person with an elevated EI then you must be able to recognize your feelings. Regulation, discipline as well as self-management are important aspects. Controlling your emotions is essential so that you can to maintain control. Self-management is also the basis of self-motivation. It is a important element to achieve any kind of accomplishment and to be able to push in tough circumstances.

The ability to recognize the feelings of others, recognize them, and develop empathy for the feelings of others is is required to be socially aware. It is also about being able to predict the way that someone's emotions influence their thinking patterns. In relation management, it is the application of social awareness capabilities. If you have an excellent ability to manage relationships then you are able to apply your knowledge of the emotions of others to seem more friendly to others.

People are more likely be drawn to you if you've got good relationships management abilities. They'll be more likely to to get in touch with them. Unfortunately, there isn't any one test to determine your EI that psychologists, and other professionals within their fields, agree to accept.

There are those who believe that there is no single method to assess an individual's EI and that the majority of its evidence is found in the person's motives and thoughts generally. There are many external factors that may influence a person's achievement. There isn't a single method of knowing exactly the extent to which one's EI can be helping or negatively hindering their progress.

To reap the benefits of this, you'll need to find new ways to improve your EI. One thing to keep in mind is the fact that you EI can be improved through the effort you make to improve it. The brain's plasticity makes this happen. The brain can modify its circuitry in addition to the strength and capacity of various components, in large part due to its plasticity. We believed that childhood was the end of all plasticity but recent research developments in recent times have proved that this isn't the reality. Children have higher brain development than adult brains, however adult brains do alter. Incorporating new habits to improve your ways of thinking and acting can yield positive results. Continuous practice will create new circuits.

To increase your self-awareness There are five areas of behavior and emotion you need to be aware of. The first is your attitude towards others. Do you notice that you are extremely critical of other people? Do you frequently insist on continuous recognition? Or do you show faith in your self? Do you strive to achieve goals at work, and do you appreciate the accomplishments and goals of coworkers? You might be amazed at how it will aid you on your way. Another aspect is your tendency to evaluate yourself. Do you think there are no flaws in you? Are you sincere about yourself? Remember that everyone has strong and weak points. It shows the strength of how you conduct yourself when can admit your shortcomings. The next area to focus on is your behaviour and reactions to situations that can be stressful. In what degree are you capable of staying in control in your emotional state, and your expression of emotions during difficult circumstances? Another aspect is whether you accept responsibility for your own errors. Do you recognize quickly that you've committed mistakes and then apologize promptly? Do you consider what other people will think about being affected by your conduct before you make a decision? One of the most important aspects of this process is to imagine yourself in someone other's shoes and act in a way you want other people to behave toward you.

Essential components of EI are self-monitoring as well as reflection. If you are truly determined to increase your EI then you have to be prepared to put in the effort and be committed to making the necessary changes. It isn't easy to change your habits, but you will discover that the outcomes will be worthy of the time and effort.

Self-regulation/Self-control

Being in control of your emotions as well as your conscious reaction to the world and not allowing your emotions to dictate your behavior.

Empathy/Understanding

This doesn't necessarily indicate that you feel the emotions of someone else however, it does mean that you have compassion for the emotions they're feeling. It also means being able to recognize the social interactions.

Assertiveness

Being able and capable of expressing your personal opinions and convictions even if they're opposed to the majority.

Persuasion

Being able to trigger specific reactions from others.

Leadership

Being able to think up ideas and inspire others with your thoughts.

Collaboration

Working with other people, in order to achieve the same goal.

Chapter 2: Being in Contact With Your Feelings

Engaging with your emotions can help you learn more about your own reactions and the world around you. Understanding what's happening within you will allow you deal with the emotions that are automatic or provoked more efficiently. This could result in a more peaceful and more relaxed daily life. It will also improve the happiness level over the long term.

Being able to recognize and be aware of emotional states in your own life can lead to an comprehension of the psychological conditions of others. This could dramatically enhance how well you interact with others both in your professional and personal lives. This chapter will cover the top emotions to be aware of, and we will go over methods to connect with them with greater efficiency.

What are emotions?

An emotion is a complicated psychological condition that consists of elements of your personal experiences physical responses, as well as behaviors. In the simplest sense, emotions are the states of mind that we can feel (both physically as well as psychologically). They are the states that manifest through changes that occur in the body (blushing is an obvious instance) and can influence our actions.

If we're in love we experience a weird feeling of tingling in our bodies when we meet the person we love. We tend to be uncoordinated, say silly things and, often, start to blush. These are emotions that are common to the majority but not all of us.

The psychological research conducted over the past decade has revealed six fundamental universal emotions. This list includes happiness surprised, sadness, disgust, fear and anger. That is to say that we all have the capacity to experience and express any of these six fundamental emotions. When we find ourselves in a situation that triggers one of these emotions within us, we're capable of feeling it and expression.

It is possible to feel angered at someone or something, especially if we feel as though something wrong has occurred to us. These emotions are known as primary emotions. Any other emotion that comes from them, therefore, is a secondary emotion.

Primary emotions

Primary emotions are the initial feelings we experience. They are the first reaction we have to a situation or incident. If someone threatens us, we may feel scared. If someone who loved us deeply and who meant an enormous amount to us passes away and we grieve, it is normal to feel sad. It is not necessary for us to dwell on them in order to feel their loss. They are instinctive reactions that we are able to feel. The seven universal feelings are the primary emotions. We have the capacity to feel them as well as react to an event or event.

However, we be unable to recognize emotions that are the most important to us and others. It is because they tend to disappear quickly when they show up. Therefore, if we don't understand our emotions, they could be overlooked and not be aware of their impact creating on our behavior.

Due to their ability to disappear quickly and disappear quickly, they are often replaced by other emotions. This makes it difficult to discern the real reason behind what's happening to us and why we're reacting to a specific situation the way we react. If we do not know our reactions to emotions and physiological triggers in depth, we can be prone to misinterpret the primary emotion. This could result in unintentional actions toward ourselves as well as unjust behavior towards others.

Secondary emotions

Secondary emotions are triggered by primary emotions. They could be a direct result of them, or be a result of more intricate chains of thought. In the first instance, the fear that is triggered by threat could transform into anger that stimulates the body with adrenalin which allows us to take action when an event requires such action from us.

However, the feelings of sadness following an end to a relationship with the person you love could turn into jealousy, because we were not able to deal with the situation in a proper way. If the ending of this relationship allows for the other to have a better life as well, we might also end up jealous of their success and happiness. That is, principal emotions such as sadness or fear can be transformed to secondary emotions like jealousy or anger.

Secondary emotions could be a basic feeling , or it could be a more complicated mix as more emotions join the mix. In the case of a breakup it is possible that the other party will be happy in the beginning since it was freedom that the person was seeking to achieve. But a sense of regret may soon arise, when one realizes the futility of the new single lifestyle.

The ability to recognize secondary emotions is equally vital (if not more so) as the ability to discern primary emotions because a reliable indicator will help us to adjust our actions and behaviors. This is one of the most crucial aspects of an emotionally intelligent behaviour that can lead to an understanding of yourself as well as in turn the other people around you. This table will assist you address the primary as well as secondary feelings:

Methods for observing emotions in Self

They are complex and without a set of skills , some basic signals about what's occurring within us may be misinterpreted or ignored. Being able to recognize your feelings, emotions and moods will greatly improve the emotional intelligence you possess. In the end, this could lead to greater satisfaction in both professional and private life, as well as greater satisfaction all around.

Self-remembering

Self-remembering is a method that can help you observe your emotions by using a technique known as"retrospection.. Retrospection literally is the word used the ability to "look in the back" and that's exactly the way to go about using it. In a more general sense, it is to examine the events that occurred during the time. Because the aim of this method is to connect with your feelings You will be watching and analyzing the emotional experiences of your personal history. This method is also employed by many psychiatrists in assessing the relationship of a patient's prior events on their current state of mind. You can now make a simplified version for yourself.

Use these steps to remember yourself:

Find a calm, peaceful location where you can unwind and not be disturbed for at least one hour.

Bring out a notebook or pen to record anything interesting you notice or recall when you are doing this exercise.

Relax or lay down to ensure you're at ease and can close your eyes.

Begin by focusing your attention on one positive emotion that is a primary one, such as love or happiness.

Reminisce about the moments in the past that you felt this feeling regardless of whether it was the tiniest bit of time.

You should try to pinpoint one moment that you have experienced in the past where this feeling was the most significant. If you can identify multiple instances, it is okay.

Write them down on your notepad.

Keep that feeling in your mind. Be completely absorbed by it.

Pay attention to every particular of that moment when the emotion was greatest. Was there anyone else? What was the location? What date was it? The sights, smells sounds and other sounds were there?

Be aware of yourself. What was that feeling like? Was your heart racing? Did you feel feelings of butterflies around your belly? What were you doing as a consequence of this emotion? Why did you behave this way? What are some other actions which you might have performed to convey the same feeling?

Then think about how that emotion is linked to the circumstance. What caused you feel so strongly? How did other people react to your actions? What do you imagine they were feeling about it? What is the reason they were feeling that way? What did you do to identify these emotions that they felt?

This exercise can give you an insight into the state of your emotions. If you conduct it correctly and with the intent to learn something new about yourself and your emotions and feelings It could be a surprise to you. You can use it to manage many different emotions, whether primary or secondary. This allows you to track your own emotional states and apply them to any future event.

The next time you notice a distinct sensation in your stomach, under the heart, you'll be certain that this is the first stage of a certain emotion. You'll also be aware of the kind of behavior you should anticipate from yourself and what impact it has on people who surround you. Self-observation although simple in nature, is able to assist you in getting into the zone of your emotions and could lead to a greater levels in emotional intelligence.

The Descriptive Experience Sampling (DES)

The retrospective method permits you to gain knowledge from your previous experiences and apply this information to your current state of mind. The method of descriptive experience, in contrast allows you to examine your present emotional states and help you be able to understand the reasons behind what you feel.

The process is more complicated than the first one, but it will assist you in increasing your awareness of your emotions and be in touch with them. It is comprised of three distinct methods which include sampling your experience randomly during the day; re-reading your notes and looking for patterns in your emotions and emotions.

1.) Recording your experience (Duration between 1 and two weeks, 7 times per day):

For you to begin savoring your own experience , you'll need an alarm or mobile application that reminds you to make a note about your current feelings 7 times per day. If your schedule doesn't permit as many times, make sure to write minimum five times per day.

The most effective method is setting your alarm to various times throughout the day.

Making it a habit to set it at different times throughout the day will ensure that you don't have to be conscious of the exact time to record it. If you keep doing it all at once it will become a routine and you'll be able to control your emotions as the time approaches.

It is also necessary to have an organized notebook to record the observations you make in. After you set five to seven alarms for the day, you are able to begin by doing the workout. Each time your alarm clock or mobile app goes off, you'll need to put down whatever you were doing in the moment and pay attention to the way you feel at that time.

Pay attention to the way you feel and experience things, not only what you feel. It is essential to write down the feelings and emotions you are experiencing at the moment, however, to truly enhance your emotional intelligence, you'll need to be able to recognize the way you feel it. By the end of the first week, your journal will have seven (or at the very least five) entries that are similar to this:

I was walking along the street. A car drove by. The driver was crazy who was driving too fast and nearly struck me. I'd like to pursue him. I feel so angry. My forehead is vibrating. I experience a strange feeling inside my abdomen. Perhaps I'm afraid. I'm breathing extremely. I almost died. It's likely to be both.

After a couple of weeks of postings similar to this (with 5-7 days per week) It is possible to move to the next step that will help you figure out the root of your feelings.

2.) Re-reading your notes (Duration 1 day)

Following the initial phase in writing your thoughts it is time to review your notes. This involves the self-remembering technique, as which was described in the preceding section. Check each entry you've created and try to recall the information.

Find out why you were feeling the way you did and how it affected your thoughts and behavior. Add any observations you've made to your notes and plan for the next week of observing. Some new observations could be like "I am so angry over the car that it brought back memories of when my dog was struck by the car when I was a child." It could be as easy as identifying the main emotional reaction (like fear) that was the source the anger.

As you begin the process over again for the next week, you should use the information you've learned about yourself thus far and be very precise. The next time you take notes, they should appear a bit more like:

I'm feeling something odd inside my stomach. It's not hungry, I've eaten. It's cold but sharp at same at the same time. I'm thinking of my girlfriend. It's possible that this feeling is linked to my thoughts. I am in love with her. It's my body telling me that I love her.

After you've completed this step, you are able to move on to the most important section of the procedure.

3) Finding patterns (Duration 1 to 2 days)

After you have completed the sampling phase of the descriptive sample of experiences, you'll be required to revisit your notes. The next time, you shouldn't be focused on every single note, rather on your personal experiences of those two weeks overall. The primary goal of this exercise is to pinpoint your emotions during a particular event and the physical or emotional feelings that are connected to these emotions.

In the beginning, you'll need to pay attention to yourself your feelings, and their connection to your actions. In addition, you'll need to pay attention to the emotions and behaviour of other people involved in the incident. If you had an employee who was furious at you when you decided to ignore him to finish your essay Try to determine why he behaved as he did and how it was that he was thinking at the moment.

In the present, it should not be difficult to accomplish. Since you're able to sense emotions within your own and other people (or that is, your emotional intelligence) should be able to make this happen. It is also possible to see how your greater emotional awareness is beginning to enhance your relationships with other people.

Chapter 3: Rise above The Herd

The most certain outcome from Emotional Intelligence will be the ability to be able to stand out from the crowd. The majority of the information in this book is derived out of the experience and wisdom senior citizens I have worked with for more than 38 years. Therefore, the subject of aging and old age is a frequent topic. They showed me that we do not all live and age the same way. Additionally, they taught me that the age of a person is simply a number that's not a direct reflection of capability or commitment.

It is possible to be old by 30 and young by the age of 80. The general rule is that self-concept and attitude are the most important aspects. According to Henry Ford once said, "If you believe that you're capable of doing something or believe you're unable to do something, then you're probably right." [3] What do you think about your self-concept? Your answer will be the determining factor in the direction you'll take in your life.

Your DNA was created for by God to be special. God incorporated your potential to differentiate based on talent in your DNA from the moment you were born by the womb of your mother. Everyone has this ability, but , unfortunately, the majority of us never discover and build it. However, you can be able to do so if you follow this book and all of the exercises that it offers. Age is not a barrier to your capacity to become the emotionally intelligent you. If you're young, the greatest is yet to be achieved. If you're old and you are old, the best is still to be. The only thing that is different is that the younger you are the longer you'll need to live a full life. Start today. One thing is certain. Whatever your age you'll never be any younger than the person you are today.

The actor John Wayne, in character as well as in real life was well-known for his blunt stance. Consider seriously this line of speech. "Life isn't easy and it's harder when you're dumb". [4] Do you not think it's foolish to have a negative self-image and the constraining impact from a herd that is stampeding create life harder for you? Herds create dust, lots of dust. It can cover you in the remnants of what other people leave behind. Stand out from the crowd.

The view is improved. There's less dust from the herd that blocks your vision, and you're no longer stuck walking along the dirt and throwing hooves of cattle in the distance. When you're above the herd and free of dust, you'll be able to determine how to go toward the top of herd. Learn more on the importance of a self-esteem and positive image in subsequent chapters. It's not clear if John Wayne studied Emotional Intelligence However, he had the concept right. Life, which is tough enough by itself, is more difficult when you're dumb.

I'm thinking of a cartoon I had in my office for a long time. It featured a group of dogs in sleds pulling a loaded sled as well as the driver. The caption read "Unless you're the lead dog, the view will never change." Do you have a view about that image? Sled dogs, at least, don't work in the shadow of dust.

Although aging is inevitable, there is no need to look or appear old. In reality, you're not old until you claim you are. Therefore, stop making complaining. I made this comment last night with my dear acquaintance Alan Jones. Without hesitation even for an instant, he glanced over his left arm the one which he tore recently muscles while when he was doing "aggressive" yardwork, and told him, "Shut up!"

In the same way, fear, especially fear of failing is normal and sometimes even healthy However, you don't have to let it prevent you from achieving your goals. Let's take a lesson the lessons of Henry Ford. "Failure is just a chance to start again with a more sophisticated approach". [5] Don't end at "I tried this once, but it failed." Try again. Take a look at a few testimonials from famous people who tried again and failed.

"Thomas Edison's teachers told him Edison was "too dumb to understand anything." Edison was dismissed at the beginning of his two careers because of having been "non-productive." Edison was an inventor. Edison attempted 1,000 times to create the bulb that lights up.

A reporter was asked "How do you feel when you be unable to complete thousand times?"

Edison replied, "I didn't fail 1,000 times. Light bulbs were invented that had 1,000 steps. " [6]

"Albert Einstein didn't speak until the age of 4 and did not learn to read until he reached the age of 7. His parents believed that he had a personality that was "sub-normal," and one of his teachers described Einstein as "mentally slow, insular and drifting through endless fantasies." He was exiled from the school and denied admission to the Zurich Polytechnic School. He did learn to read and speak. Even to do a little math."[7]

Fred Smith, the founder of Federal Express, received a "C" on his college assignment that detailed his concept for an overnight delivery service that was reliable and secure. His teacher at Yale advised him "Well, Fred, the idea is intriguing and well-thought out, but for it to be able to earn more than an "C" grade Your ideas must also be able to be practical. [8]

It seems that some of the most well-known and successful people on the planet were born with the group. It's not where you begin but where you finish that is important. Remember that the herd isn't happy to witness anyone break free and fly. The herd will stop you from flying. in place.

A lot of what we experience is the result of choices we've made. choices that are restricted due to uncontrollable and unreasonable fear. This book is designed to assist you in putting these kinds of decisions over. Don't be just a follower. Be an innovator. There's a reason someone has to do it. So why shouldn't you? Therefore, if after reading this book, you discover ways to make fresh and better decisions I'll be happy. If not, go back and read the book over. The clues were not there!!

"Ever tried. Never failed. Whatever the reason. Retry. Refuse to fail. Fail more often."

Samuel Beckett

Naturally, I would like readers to read this book from beginning to finish. I did, in fact have spent 38 years collecting the data , and then spending a number of lengthy months writing it. I don't want anyone to think I was wasting my time.

I'm sure that pleasing me, regardless of how happy it might be for me, isn't enough of a reason to continue reading.

Let me give you an agreement. This is an excellent one:

I can assure you that If you take the time to read this book, agree with its basic premise and follow the principles it lays out, you'll be able to move toward the front of the herd and receive the following benefits:

A greater sense of goal

A clear idea of what your dream life could be and the specific goals to get it done

Fitness, health and more energy

Optimism allows you to spot and capitalize on opportunities

The ability to harness the energy of your emotions to shape your future

The satisfaction of knowing that you are appreciated and making an impact

A sharper mind

Financial security

Engaging relationships

Development of your leadership skills as a leader

You have the ability to live your life as the most ideal version of yourself

The combination of the following ten ingredients into your personal mix will result in the Emotionally intelligent You.

Determine Your Mission and Goal. You were created for excellence. Find it. Follow it. Do it. Take it on. Make yourself the person you are intended to be. Paul, the apostle Paul writes in 1 Corinthians 12 and in Romans 12 make clear that in our creation as a human being the Holy Spirit gave us particular talents, or gifts which were intended to be cultivated, developed, and refined as we mature. It is significant that in the past, scientists recognized that embedded in your DNA are the propensities to excel in specific, particular areas. Additionally both science and Bible confirm that our talents abilities are exclusive to us as individuals. It is within these talent propensities that our potential for greatness is located. Find them, and begin working to be great.

Make the most of Your Future. Begin with a big dream. Create your Vision, then set goals, keep your focus and leave a lasting impression. Every person needs a powerful dream, a big one that is clear and quantifiable as to the reason you take on the tasks you undertake. Take this quote as an example: "When your why is sufficient, you'll determine your method." Les Brown. Also, in other terms, if the motivation that we are motivated to accomplish the goal we want to achieve isn't compelling enough, or isn't strong enough to inspire us to take decision-making, every actions we take will be in a haphazard manner and weak at the very least. Author and speaker Jack Canfield says, "Successful people keep a positive perspective throughout their lives regardless of the circumstances within them." 11. My good friend and mentor

Steve Duba, frequently reminds me, "The biggest impediment to success is having a broken focus." Start by establishing a vision. Then, you can move your dream into a the vision. From your vision, set goals. And then, follow these goals with unstoppable, determined focus. As you do you'll leave the foundation of positive experiences and memories that have a far greater value than the sum of cents and dollars.

Enhance your Opportunities with an optimistic attitude. I like Optimism. I love optimism but have come to the realization that unbalanced optimism can quickly transform into illusion. So, face today's realities, but remain in your dreams. Plan for better days. In addition, Optimists live up to 8 years longer than pessimists. So, I would guess that they have better health. Positive attitude is a reflection of an open mind and ready to come up with solutions, whereas the pessimist sees only barriers.

Let loose the power of your emotions to gain positive results. Many have built nearly impermeable emotional barriers around themselves. These walls were designed to shield the person from physical and emotional hurt, they, in reality turn into chains of failure, which hold the person behind. Remove those chains and, in doing so you'll be adding quality and quantity to your life. Learn and practice the four foundations of Emotional intelligence, self-awareness, Social-Awareness, Self-Control, and Management of Relationships. Think about this quote: believe that imagination can be more powerful than knowledge. The power of mythology is greater than the past. The power of dreams is greater than the facts. Hope always wins over experiences. The only thing that can be cured is laughter. cure for sorrow. I also am convinced that love is stronger than death. Robert Fulghum[1212

Maintain and strengthen your body through a balanced and balanced program of resistance and aerobic training. Encourage physical fitness within your own life and then in the lives of the people you love. Aerobic exercise improves endurance, while resistance training strengthens muscles and helps strengthen bones. You'll become stronger and more active. At times, you could be sick however not as frequently or for longer than you could currently be suffering from. You'll appear healthier, feel better and be able to accomplish more. Think about these thoughts: "Those who think they don't have time for physical fitness will sooner or later be forced to take time to deal with illnesses" The Edward Stanley

Engage, Take Part Engage, Participate, and make a positive impact throughout your Life. If you're not one yet It is highly unlikely that you'll become an active social butterfly. However, you can make things happen instead of looking around and wondering what has happened. You'll feel a greater feeling of being useful and wanted. In addition, you will and will make a huge positive impact on the lives of all those you interact with. There's an old yet very true cliche which says "If you want to change it the case, it's my decision." The idea is that when you don't feel satisfied with the way you're feeling, take action and be accountable for making the change you'd like to see take place. The majority of people don't realize this, but you'll If you haven't already.

Be able to withstand stress, anxiety and loss with the power of Meditation, Prayer and Humor as well as an intimate connection to the higher power you already have a relationship with as God. Through this process you will notice improvements in your health and see your feelings of peace, security, and safety grow. A key aspect of happiness is stressed in the following quote"Laughter can be described as the sunshine that snatches away winter's sting. Victor Hugo[13]

Engage with People who energize and inspire you, and who are inspired and energized by You. Be more caring and less unreliable. There is a saying that you are and will never be more that the standard of the people whom you are friends with. A world-class speaker and author, Orrin Woodward says it this way. "Show me the lives of the five most influential people you hang out with, and I'll tell you the direction your life is heading." Do you confident that you want to live all your life where the majority of your acquaintances are? Are your people a source of joy for you or do they make you feel down? In other words, are you an energy source for your acquaintances, or do you drain the water out of them? A relationship that isn't defined by the sharing of energy and encouragement is not one that should be a place where a lot of time be spent.

Set up Sound Strategies to Achieve Time and Financial Freedom. There's a saying that goes, "Time is money." I'd like to add "And the process of making money takes time." The majority of people, I've noticed wake up early in the morning, and then head into a job they do not like, and they swap their time for cash. As a result is that time has gone and the money frequently not enough. (My dad used to say there was a lot of time remaining at the conclusion of his savings.) In addition, the constant exchange of our time and money for cash hardly ever results in the realization of our hopes. The economic elements are all against us. There's a financial spider web (I'll explain more details about this web in the future) that traps you in debt chains easy credit, minimal down payments, and seemingly interminable times to repay the loans. This means that our time and money are taken away from us. Unfortunately, 90 percent of Americans have credit cards and more than half are in debt over their heads. Take on the web. The web's woven strands can be tempting but slick, strong chains made of industrial strength Velcro that are securing you and placing you in a very dangerous position. Take the chains off. Be financially free and regain your time. It's possible to fulfill your life without having to take on. It is possible to gain the time you've spent. All you need is the willingness to put off the moment, create a strategy to earn more money and, most importantly, take care of yourself first, and then put aside the money you've spent. Learn to think as an entrepreneurial person. I'll teach you how with Chapter 13.

Enhance the capacity of your mind. Explore, Experiment, Learn, Grow. Your Brain needs a place to call home in a strong, healthy body, fueled by proper nutrition and regular exercise. Explore and experiment. While you will be able to learn and experiment with new ideas and be inspired to do it and love doing it. In the end, keep in mind that your brain requires an environment that is healthy for it to flourish and grow within. There is an indestructible link between an energised body and a well-functioning brain. Learning new things, coupled with exercising that you love is the way to generate neuronal cells (Neuro-genesis) in order to take over the tens of thousands who die from natural causes every single day. They also create new pathways in your brain (Neuro-Plasticity) in the event that circumstances like strokes or other strokes have affected your clarity of thought.

It may sound like an enormous amount of information to be gleaned from a short book and it actually is. I don't blame you if you are at this point in your journey and have some doubts. What I can provide you at this moment in these words to you, is this. I've tried everything I can recommend and it's all working for me. I'm fairly average, so If these principles have worked for me, I can see no reason why they shouldn't be effective for you.

But don't simply believe me when I say so. Learn some important lessons from those who survived well. In a research study of about 169 individuals older than 100, the following patterns of life were observed in the majority. Note that there are some similarities between this lists and the 10 points I have just mentioned.

Age-related people are:

Positive attitudes, but with little evidence of depression

A strong ability to deal with loss and stress

Regular and rigorous intellectual stimulation

The utilization of humor as a way to cope

A robust social network that provides interaction and help

There are a few instances of obesity, overuse of cigarettes or alcohol healthy is another way of saying

While reading this book, you'll see additional illustrations for the examples, and several more. This has previously been done. Why wouldn't you want to? Many people are living well and in good health frequently into their 80s. What's stopping you? Why are you unable to make the choice to be you are the emotionally smart person? Do you fear change, or do you feel it's too late for you to make the make a change?

It's a well-worn cliche that is like this. "You cannot make an old dog learn new tricks."

Now, you may think "I'm an elderly dog, and it's way too late to be able to adapt. Don't give up. take a look at this tale of a dog who learned, until the end of his life numerous new tricks in opposition to any expert's knowledge, opinion and judgement. This is a tale of an actual old dog.

My best close friends Kevin as well as Jodie have a love for dogs. In all honesty, Jodie loves dogs; Kevin is a lover of Jodie So, Kevin accepts dogs (Now this is an example of Emotional intelligence in a marriage. Kevin is my favorite.) typically between five and six at a time , sharing his home and eating food.

Not too long ago, in order to protect the dog from being killed, Jodie took in an old dog called Joe. Experts advised Jodie to ensure that Joe was comfortable until he passed away. Jodie was too old, deaf, blind, and suffering from a heart murmur that was advanced to be of any benefit.

It's not just that Jodie love dogs, but she frequently doesn't follow directions well She isn't always a good listener! She took Joe home and introduced him to her companions in the house (and Kevin, who had resigned Kevin) and took him the home. Leash-trained, she took from room to room and he was awed! She explained the meaning behind the word cookie by hand signals.

In the final season of life Joe was an established local star and was often accompanied by Jodie on public appearances promoting the benefits of adopting senior dogs. While he wasn't performing on the speaking circuit, Old Joe raced around the house, effortlessly keeping pace with young dogs and frequently racing around Kevin. Stairs were only minor hurdles and he would beg food at the table along with the very best of them.

Sure, Joe was an old dog, and more than the majority of you who read about Joe. However, love, perseverance, determination and gentle training helped him learn new techniques. In his last year, the man lived his most fulfilling life and was awed by it. You too can live the way the old Joe did. You might appear to be old after a while or an old dog in mind but you can master new techniques. In his new house and even in his last year, the blind and deaf Joe was able to stand out from the crowd. You too can.

Chapter 4: Relating emotions

Human brains are constantly engaged. It's not built to cease. There aren't any situations that our brain asks us to take a break. If it ever does stop for a moment the brain would be dead. We are always working no matter if we're asleep eating, or relaxing, or taking an exam.

In the same way, our emotions make us cognizant of them at every day in our daily lives. Feelings and emotions behave as wives. They have made it a daily habit to send us brain messages every day to ensure that they're the ones that we return home and not ...That's an article for another day.

Feelings are powerful emotions, that result from the circumstances, situations such as social influence, everyday pressures, social reactions and interactions. They can be described as any kind of conscious experience that is the result of extreme joy or disappointment. The elements that increase our feelings are our temperament, mood as well as our personality and motivation. Remember, these are merely factors that increase our feelings. These aren't real emotions.

It is easy to determine the emotion that has taken over our bodies, since they give us signs. For instance, if you're scared that you will sweat and shake, which is followed by a faster heartbeat. If you're shy you might notice your blood rushing onto your cheeks.

It is true that emotions are an unsolved issue. Endocrinology, neuroscience, psychology and medicine, as well as sociology, history and computer science each of these disciplines has conducted numerous research studies on human emotions. This is an indication of how important this subject. The most accurate and general definition we could give for this elusive term is that emotions are reactions to significant external and internal elements.

There are many emotions that we experience throughout the day. Every one of us is a distinct person and therefore, we experience various emotions in every circumstance. We may start the day feeling angry at our alarmsand rush to "snoozing" the alarm until we realise that another delay could result in being fired. Others start their day with a smileand having a good time and feeling content, anticipating a fun day ahead.

The idea is the fact that feelings are distinct to each person, and it is important to be able to interpret them in a way that is appropriate for you.

Emotional Intelligence

What is emotional intelligence? John Mayer and Peter Salavoy came up with"Emotional Intelligence" or "Emotional Intelligence" or EI to describe the capacity to recognize, understand and manage our own emotions as well as the emotions of those around us. The people with greater emotional intelligence find it very simple to manage and respond to situations. Additionally, they find it simple to maintain and develop relationships because of their ability to recognize and handle the emotions of others. They can also shield themselves from depression and stress since they are aware of methods for managing their emotions.

Some of us might begin to dwell on the fact that we're not emotionally smart and all of the above points don't apply to us. We must eliminate this naive notion out of our minds and accept the reality we're about to learn.

While it's true that some individuals are born with an emotional intelligence and others don't however, you can more emotionally intelligent by simply focusing on and developing the required skills.

How do I Feel?

We've come to understand that emotional intelligence refers to the ability to detect and manage our own emotions as well as those of others who surround us. One good inquiry to make is something along the lines of "How do you identify one's emotions?"

Here are a few methods of doing this:

Through examining your physical reaction. Let's suppose that someone is talking with you face-to-face and then says something that is negative about you. In the event that your palm suddenly leaps in the air, and then lands directly on their face and you see their face, you'll realize that you're not just angry, but have a deep hatred for the person. The human body is an amazing thing. It operates in a stunning pattern that needs to be comprehended. Once we have it figured out, we are able to effortlessly and effectively take control of it. It is the control that is at stake in every aspect of life. Learn about your body and reactions. Take a close look at it and make notes in your mind.

Listening to the music you enjoy. Are you aware of how you are feeling at this moment? Turn on your music device and select a tune. The song will let you know precisely what you feel. If you're unhappy, you'll never be listening to Taylor Swift! Instead, you're likely to sing a soothing and soothing sad track that allows you to remain in the present. Once you've noted the feelings you are experiencing, say to yourself "That is not the way I feel."

Talk with someone. Speak to someone near to you. Share your feelings with them and let them be able to understand your feelings. This will help you gain an entirely different perspective that can help you recognize your emotions and figure out solutions for them. It will also make you feel much more peaceful once you've poured your heart into someone.

The process of recognizing emotions is an uphill endeavor. At night, you might be feeling empty in your soul, making you feel weak and weak. Try to comprehend it. You consider your previous relationships, your relationship with your spouse as well as your family and that new employer at work, but you aren't able to pinpoint the reason you feel empty. On the next day, however you discover a chocolate bar in your cupboard, when the initial bite the chocolate fills the empty space within your heart, bringing you a sense of sweet happiness.

Humans aren't particularly complex. We only make ourselves appear complex without any reason!

Chapter 5: The art of Self-Confidence

Self-confidence can be defined as a belief in your capabilities, abilities and judgment. Self-confidence is achieved when we have attained proficiency in a specific area or field. If we feel confident that we are confident that we will be able to manage any circumstance in the future.

Self-confidence differs from self-esteem. Self-confidence is based on trusting the ability of you to accomplish your objectives, self-esteem is akin to the way in which you see your self-worth. It is crucial to remember that not all people are confident in themselves. The majority of great leaders you have heard of had a lack of confidence in their abilities. In reality, self-confidence is all about the mind. Self-confidence needs to be practiced and developed before you will attain it.

How to build confidence in yourself

Here are six ways to boost your confidence:

Make your body learn your language with confidence. The first thing observed about a person will be the way they look. It is the most simple aspect to detect and will immediately let people know whether you are confident or unsecure. are. Imagine yourself as an confident person and you'll feel comfortable. Your body language speaks to people that you have confidence in yourself, they will begin to respect your confidence and view you as an individual of great worth. In the workplace the boss will grant you the power to control things by placing you in charge of a certain task or project. A confident body language helps a person feel more in control. Straight shoulders, firm handshakes as well as eye contact and maintaining a consistent voice enhances your body language, and will make you appear confident.

Dress with confidence. However sad this reality is, we're all aware of what our initial impression is simply by looking at the mirror. Many people are aware that their clothes and appearance are "checked over" and consequently, they shudder and lose confidence. To counter this negative feeling be sure to dress properly. It's not necessary to wear extravagant clothes to impress others! Wear something you are confident makes you feel confident about yourself. Select clothes that match your mood, personality, and style. If you wish to portray an aura of accomplishment wear a dress to show your success. If you are comfortable in the clothes you've put on, you'll feel comfortable in them. If you are having trouble engaging in conversations with bold jewelry or ties, these are great ways to start conversations. Wearing a stylish outfit will help you feel comfortable in your skin and, consequently, create a feeling of absolute confidence.

Confidence in your speech. Visit YouTube and look for inspirational speakers. Choose your favourite among them Take some time to look at how they talk and ask yourself what you love most about them. Be aware of how they look at the audience, the way they emphasize certain words; how their tone changes every now and then in response to the audience's interest; and how they seem relaxed, steady, and natural in their speech. Pay attention to everything about them and then try to emulate every one of those things. Make sure you are assertive when dealing with others, since when you speak with confidence and confidently, you also boost your self-esteem. It is important to let your serious leader to shine from within your own self. Don't sway, raise your voice, or talk during your speech. Make sure you are serious about your speech and the audience will be able to follow.

Be optimistic. Make a conscious decision to base all of your actions and actions on positive thinking. Keep your mind focused and remind yourself that you're a confident person and you will soon feel the confidence that surrounds you. Beware of all negative thoughts, individuals of ideas, and thoughts, and keep your mind solely on the positive aspects. Negativity robs the confidence you have. Keep your positive attitude by smiling frequently by thinking of positive thoughts, and surrounding yourself with positive and content people. It will also boost confidence in yourself, but also keep you satisfied and happy.

Be confident. Once you've learned the importance of being confident and feeling confident, immediately begin to act that way. Take off your chicken costume, and get out and make eye contact with strangers! Take on those work-related targets and jobs you'd normally dismiss. You can take an unintentional leap of faith and assure yourself you'll be able to do it. Do your best to be confident in yourself and you will reach a point that confidence will become second nature to you. Discover what your strengths as well as weaknesses are and try to keep them in the forefront. Discover your strengths and work to overcome your weaknesses.

Prepare yourself. If you're prepared, nothing will take you off guard. If you are prepared confidence will come in and you will not have to deal with any surprises. Everything flows smoothly and since you're aware of all that has taken place or is about to take place, you're completely confident about your work and actions. This can help increase confidence in yourself. Find out everything you can know about your job and the business you run. By perseverance and patience, you will gain self-confidence.

Chapter 6: Eq Versus Iq

The IQ and EQ issue came into existence after Dan Goleman introduced emotional intelligence. Many psychologists say that IQ alone is insufficient until a person has an equivalent EQ which lets them interact with one another. The EQ stands for emotional intelligence quotient and refers to the ability of a person to discern emotions, utilize emotions, comprehend emotions, and manage emotions in themselves as well as others. It is what gives understanding and depth to connections. There isn't a fixed relationship among IQ as well as EQ (you may have both the same, however it is possible to be a person with an EQ that is high EQ and a low IQ and reverse).

Although IQ is the main control, EQ could be described to be an engineer that understands how to repair these cables when one fails either here or elsewhere. It increases the ability to recover quickly and easily from the ravages of external forces. This is why you can find compassionate individuals who tend to be more open and understanding of their counterparts and enjoy long-lasting relationships. If you have two individuals with extremely excellent levels of EQ They are likely to more stable than the rest of us. They not only connect, but they also know how to ensure their connections are secure.

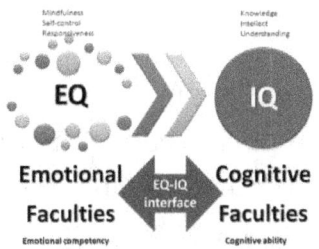

Relations between cognitive and emotional faculties

Cognitive faculties such as knowledge understanding and intellect are essential in making decisions and 80percent of people rely on them to make daily life-related decisions. The higher your education, the more reliant you are on the cognitive process. It is at this point that your choices start to go wrong because pure cognition isn't the main thing in life. Life is more complex and the cognitive faculties are interspersed with emotions that are the heart of our minds. The faculties of the emotional mind, such as mindfulness reflection, self-control, compassion, empathy, and understanding requirements of others, etc. form the emotional faculties that matter to success in life.

This is the an extremely powerful way to influence the performance. It connects the faculties of emotional and cognitive and abilities to enhance the process of making decisions and the operational performance of an individual.

The concept of emotional intelligence is thought to play a significant part in modern business environment. Its concepts aid in evaluating and influencing the behavior of business people as well as managerial styles, attitudes as well as interpersonal abilities and potentials and is thought to have immense significance in areas such as hiring, profiling hiring and selection. Business professionals or managers who are successful do not waste their time or energy thinking about how they can be superior to others They focus on being the best person they can be. Another benefit of having an emotional intelligence is that it helps people overcome and get over the fears and challenges that they confront and prevents them from moving forward and seeking out the appropriate kind of assistance. It helps to understand your own behavior as well as the relationship one has with other people. Studies in psychology have proven that

"The best job is the one who can get it accomplished without wasting time or resolving to excuses. "Napoleon Hill

Understanding and managing emotions play a an important role in satisfying one's workplace and life. In a team-based environment, those who have greater EI can influence others' moods so that they will be capable of boosting their own and the morale of their employees. They believe in the power of motivation and creativity . They are firmly convinced that they can create their own destiny. They realize that if they don't, somebody else will be deciding their destiny and future. They are open to emotions and blend their thoughts with emotions in a reflective manner, and monitor their emotions, and utilize them to determine the way to achievement rather than as a cause of conflict. They think up new concepts, think in fresh ways, are creative and enhance "big-picture" thinking, and possess improved decision-making skills. Life isn't about learning to weather the storm, but rather dancing when it rains.

People who have good EI abilities are more effective professionally and capable of making positive changes at work because they can manage emotional information in a creative manner and efficiently, especially in relation to the processing, perception understanding, management, and control of emotions. They recognize that the precious stone is not able to be polished with friction, nor is it possible to perfect without the need for trials. Highly skilled pilots earn their fame through storms and storms.

What are the best ways to make the right decisions?

There is a significant connection between feeling, emotion and decision-making. A lack of emotion can result in an impairment in decision making. When we make a decision on the basis of emotion, we need to assess the significance of our current decisions, using emotions and cognitive processes. When faced with complicated and contradicting options and options, it is possible that we are unable to make a decision using only our the cognitive process, which could be overwhelmed and not assist us in making decisions. In these scenarios, the use of physical markers can aid us in making decisions.

Somatic markers are actually interactions between reinforcing stimuli which cause an associated physiological state. In the brain, these markers are believed to be processed by the frontal region of the brain, which is known as ventromedial prefrontal cortex. Somatic marker associations could be recurrent during decision-making, and can influence how we process information. When faced with difficult and uncertain choices the somatic markers generated from the stimuli relevant to us are added into a total somatic state. The overall state influences our choice of the best way to behave. The impact on our decision-making processes could be unconsciously triggered by the ventral striatum and brainstem or conscious, using higher-cortical cognitive processing. Scientist Damasio believes that the somatic markers guide our attention to more beneficial options, which can simplify the process of making decisions.

There are some decisions that do not require conscious thinking (the decision to sleep, choice to eat, avoiding the leg from getting stuck in the door) and those that require conscious thought (decisions within social groups as well as engineering design) however they all rely in the same mechanism. For those that require conscious thinking, complexity and uncertainty, the IQ-EQ interface plays a significant importance on physical markers.

Emotions are the changes that occur in both the brain and body states as a result of different stimuli. Changes in the body's physiology (e.g. muscle tone and cardiac rate, hormone release facial expression, posture, etc.).) are triggered in the body. They are then transmitted to the brain, where they become emotions that inform the person something about the event they've encountered. As time passes emotions and the corresponding physical change(s) are correlated with specific events and their previous outcomes.

In making decisions for the future bodily signals (or "somatic markers") and the evoked emotions are either unconsciously or consciously connected with their previous outcomes and can influence decisions towards certain actions while avoiding other. For example, if an somatic marker that is that is associated with a positive outcome is observed, the individual might feel happy and encourage the person to follow the desired behavior. When a marker of the somatic type that is that is associated with a negative outcome is noticed by the person, they might feel depressed and set off an internal alarm that warns

" Everyone says they want the freedom of being free. Get the train off the tracks for free, but it's not going everywhere.

Zig Ziglar

individuals to steer clear of the individual from taking a particular course of the individual to avoid a course of action. These somatic states specific to the context that are influenced by, and strengthened through past experiences assist to steer behavior in the direction more beneficial decisions and are therefore adaptive.

The different pathways activate markers of the body. In the first emotional responses can be triggered by changes that occur in the body which are transmitted to the brain, referred to as the. For example, an object that is feared, such as snakes could trigger the fight-or-flight reaction and trigger anxiety. In the second way the cognitive representations of emotions are activated in the brain without being initiated by a physiological response, referred to as the"as-if body loop"|. For instance, the thought of the possibility of encountering snakes would trigger the same response of flight or fight as if you were actually in that circumstance (albeit maybe a weaker one). This means that the brain is able to anticipate anticipated physical changes that allow the person to respond more quickly to stimuli from outside without waiting for the event to happen.

It was discovered that patients suffering from frontal lobe injuries could produce an underlying skin conductance response to "startle" just like normal patients. However, patients with frontal lobe damage didn't show any skin conductance images. One patient observed that he was aware of the images could be disturbing, but there was no feeling of discomfort - the picture was disturbing but he did not feel. In the gambling tests, frontal lobe affected patients tended to select the high gain/high risk option, and continued to lose as a result, while normal players tended to choose the low risk/low gain option in order to get net gains. This in combination with the inverted variation of the game proved that patients with frontal lobe injuries weren't just not sensitive to punishment, but also had acquired myopia for the next.

Further studies combining gambling games with the response of the skin to conductance. Normal and frontal lobe damaged patients produced the skin conductance response when every reward and punishment was awarded. Normal subjects were able to develop (acquired) an increased skin conductance response before choosing the risky options and frontal lobe

the patients suffering from damage showed no anticipatory reaction whatsoever.

the business world.

Many industrial psychologists believe IQ emotional intelligence and its various capacities can result in better performance that makes us feel valued by others and even more respected by ourselves. It's a reward we want and can lead to increased self-confidence that could be the reason for the gap between feeling awe-inspiring and being unmotivated. Your self-perception is a huge impact on how other people perceive your self. Self-confidence is the key to happiness in your life. It is your own judgment and is directly related to your chance of success and being content. Happiness can be described as a mental or emotional state that is characterized by pleasant or positive emotions and is often considered to be the end of the road for both personal and professional lives. It is an important aspect of emotional intelligence that ranges from happiness to extreme happiness. A

A range of psychological, biological and philosophical influences contribute the way to success and happiness and have been associated with mood, personality, as well as cognition. People who are happy have the highest productivity and are highly valued throughout the world.

It is the only factor that can guarantee 50-60% achievement in life, while the remaining success is contingent on emotional intelligence as well as other elements like motivation, wealth of parents and education level and parental status, rank in the sibling hierarchy mental health, physical well-being, personality, the sign of the stars, for instance. The evidence supporting the efficacy of EI is growing more convincing. The tangible, learnable abilities of emotional intelligence have an enormous impact on organizational performance. Many people believe the importance of emotional intelligence crucial to the leaders of top-performing organisations as they strive to grow in an ever-changing and competitive market.

"The determination to succeed, the drive to be successful, the desire to realize your full potential These are the keys to let you in to personal achievement." Eddie Robinson

Entrepreneurship is not a topic that's discussed as survival, but that's precisely the definition and it's the thing that encourages creativity. The first time I ran a shop, it taught me that business isn't financial science, but rather trading, buying and selling.

Chapter 7: The Emotional Health Children

The ability to manage emotions is associated with a variety of positive outcomes. Healthy children are more resilient and have better relationships; they can deal well with the challenges of life. A child who is emotionally healthy can be found with anyone he meets himself. They're incredibly lively with their friends, radiating enthusiasm that parents of other children would like to emulate. They are able to recognize their emotions , and thus are more adept at identifying appropriate strategies to manage emotional situations. They know when it is safe to walk away, and when it's acceptable to resist.

Increase academic and learning achievement

If you have a well-tuned emotional quotient, a child's brain is at peace that allows him to remain focused to achieve a higher academic performance. Being emotionally smart allows children to concentrate and block out distractions that could be a result of emotions. In other words emotional intelligence is a significant contributor in a child's capacity to face academic challenges.

In the words of Goleman (2005) "helping youngsters to improve their self-awareness, confidence and self-confidence as well as manage their emotional turmoil and impulses, and improve their empathy will pay off not only in better behavior , but also in the improvement of their academic performance."

It could help reduce the amount of bullying.

The act of bullying is a result of a very low levels of emotional quotient. These bullies make decisions and act without considering the impact of their actions on their peers and those surrounding them. They're not in better in charge of their own feelings, and are always looking to take advantage of vulnerable people by asserting their dominance over innocent children. They are in every school, and across all levels. The majority of them are influential in school or class as they are physically stronger or more mature than their peers. This, combined with an insufficient emotional quotient causes them to channel their emotions and their privileges in a negative way. With the right emotional intelligence, this negative mental attitude will be largely eradicated in children.

Improve social effectiveness

When you have Emotional Intelligence it's easier to communicate with people at the core level. The interpersonal relationships are also significantly enhanced. Thus, people tend to be more close to one another in social situations since emotional intelligence can improve the perception of others who surround them.

Reduced risk of engaging in destructive personal actions

Children with a positive emotional intelligence are positive in their thinking. The likelihood of engaging into destructive and antisocial behavior is significantly reduced since they are able to discern their values and preferences when they reach a certain age. Children who are emotionally intelligent are accustomed to setting goals regardless of the smallest of goals. Our society will be more prosperous when children are taught the right way through life.

Chapter 8: Moving Toward The Positive

I've spoken a lot lately about resetting our minds. It could be the wrong word to employ since the idea is that it means we have set our minds at all times that we did not accomplish by ourselves. Instead of actively developing our thinking process, we generally develop the reactions we have to the different situations that we face in every day life. What we do with those situations and circumstances is usually not considered and our reactions could be more instinctual than planned. The problem is that we are more reliant on the negative thinking and reaction mechanisms, which, as I've stated are the most typical human way of dealing with issues. We are more attentive to what we put in our breakfast cereal bowls as opposed to what we think about in our minds over our lives. Of course, there are those whose outlook on life has been influenced by traumatizing incidents which may have occurred several years ago.

We seem to let the negative overpower the positive. To begin to be positive, we have to reverse this process. It may be difficult initially, since our minds constantly throw negativity at us because that is the natural response mechanism. The first step we must to be in the habit of looking at our thoughts and distinguishing among the optimistic and negative. This is an eye-opening experience as we are able to see, often in awe, how most thought patterns are negative. In the beginning, you'll likely be bombarded with thoughts about how futile it is to changing your thoughts. As our minds revert back to their comfortable negative state, we begin to observe how they operate in a state of their individual independent devices. I often find myself in disputes with other individuals, shop assistants employers, etc. with whom I'm scheduled to meet. My thoughts will go through every possible negative scenario and the way I can beat the conflict I've made up in my head. However, it is true that in nearly all cases, the conflict never happens. It was just a defense method that my mind put itself through in order to prepare in case the worst occurs. You will find that the creation of scenarios for disasters is among the most powerful abilities of the negative thinker.

When we've been astonished by the number of negative thoughts that we generate and have learned to recognize these thoughts, we can start an attack. We must learn ways to block negative thought before they begin to take hold. It's not simple to erase any negative thoughts. The mind will create a new thought and since there is an abundance of negativity to choose from, the odds are that the thought has negative connotations. We must switch it over to positive thoughts. The objective here is not only to block out negative thoughts, but to create a positive mindset as the default mindset which your mind drifts into when it is not being monitored. It is not my intention to suggest that this is effortless, but with some discipline, it can occur and the benefits you get in terms of mental peace are priceless. As time passes, we'll be able to identify the moment when negative thoughts begin to arise and be able to counter them with positive ones.

You'll need to learn to recognize situations that cause negative thinking and then take the necessary steps to avoid these situations or begin to think positively prior to the negative thoughts start to develop. One of the most common situations that trigger negativity is driving through dense traffic. Driving is the only circumstance in which I am able to be certain that anyone in my path is a moron and every person behind me is a moron. When I am in negative thinking, the possibility I could even think someone is a moron or stupid isn't even thought of to me. It is only necessary to take a look at how certain people act in the midst of traffic to see how stressful creating it is. We all have to drive, but if we recognize that it can disrupt our peaceful thinking, then we're in a position to ensure that our minds remain calm. When we accept that some of us that are out there will behave like idiots and that there's no way to prevent it, we can take a breather and accept that even though we can't control the flow of traffic, but we can influence what we do with it. Take a deep breath along with some relaxing music and a moment to concentrate on something good that happened in your day, and you'll find that the journey isn't as awful as you thought and especially when you give in on the reality that regardless of what you believe that you will not be able to be able to travel any faster than the weather allows.

Beyond just providing counter-points will be the following step. It is important to begin speaking positively, too. If we are with people, the conversation is likely to turn negative at some point. People are likely to start complaining about someone or something. This is due to the fact that, just like the person you were you were those you're speaking to have minds full of negative thoughts. The new person you're trying to build is expected to bring positive energy in the conversations. It's not as difficult as it might sound. If someone expresses an opinion that is negative, you can simply flip the argument around and present a an optimistic perspective. It's not necessary to be a polarizing or combative person It's enough to come up with something positive to share. People who had a habit of the more negative and cynical persona you used to be might be stunned when you leave the room well-dressed in a positive attire However, they'll adapt and if they don't, then go to the next step.

This leads me to my next suggestion. Be careful not to surround yourself with people who think negatively. Positive energy feeds positive energy. People who are negative drain your energy and push you back to your old habits. If possible, stay clear of them and if you are unable to, ensure that you hold more closely to your positive outlook. We can be easily influenced by people who are around us. It is a normal human instinct to want to be accepted and be part of a community which usually requires a consensus with their way of thinking and speak. This is a normal way of thinking. that when negative remarks are voiced, they are quickly amplified by those who agree. Making a statement that is in opposition to the spirit of this unity requires some courage initially and could be perceived as uncomfortable since most of us are taught to join the crowd, rather than oppose it. The reality is that people take notice of the positive sentiments and the entire flow of conversation could change. I believe this is due to the fact that, most of the time most of negative comments are not necessarily felt in the deepest sense, but is simply a second-guessing position adopted by those with a negative outlook in any discussion. A positive outlook could be easily picked up.

In our negative mental state, we were able to catastrophize things that we think about. We can blow up seemingly innocuous situations and make it the specter of a catastrophe. This is not surprising considering the environment we live in. If it weren't for the looming catastrophes, I believe that the majority of journalists would cease to exist. Sometimes it's helpful to look back and see the many earth-shaking cataclysmic events didn't take place. In 1999, we were receiving reports that, at midnight, on December 31st December, every computer on this planet would suddenly cease functioning, which would send us into an Armageddon similar to fate. When you look back, the whole story now appears ridiculous. Take a look back at some of the issues you had anticipated in your own life , which were either not even realized or turned out to be much less traumatic than you thought they were going to be. If you are able to analyze your thoughts , you'll be able to be able to see this as a behavioural habit that is often displayed when we aren't disciplined towards thinking more positive.

For some , personalizing can be an issue. They consider any issue that happens as due to their behavior or inadequate way in which they act. The self-perception they have of themselves usually began in their early years and has been carried around with them throughout their lives. It's a risky mental state to cling to as it is self-fulfilling. If someone constantly tells that to themselves "Oh I'm not able to stand up and speak before the public audience" then the chances that they'll fail when asked to speak in public is much more likely. People who have a low self-esteem are prone to negative thoughts. Yet, they are also the ones who could benefit the most from a shift in mindset.

There are people with this mindset that is deeply embedded, there are many areas that we consider as insufficient or less likely be successful. The power of our mind that it is highly unlikely that we achieve success in these vulnerable areas unless we recognize them and then replace the negativity with good ones.

Positive thinking that is forced can produce significant effects in these situations. Be disciplined in your thinking processes so that you be the person you wish to become and not who you think yourself as. Do not use words like "I cannot accomplish the job." Instead, replace these with words like "I cannot do it at the moment." Focus your thoughts on positive images that you would be in requisite scenario. If you are the first to read this article, most of you will be hesitant from what is written because your mind is flooded with negativity about changing the most vulnerable and weak areas of your life. Prepare yourself for this , and acknowledge you are experiencing a negative thought and will have to be drowned out by positive thinking.

A very effective methods to develop positive thoughts is gratitude. Prior to trying to change our mindset, we would drift around in our lives absorbing all negative experiences that are around us and happen to us, while ignoring the many wonderful things we see each day. Finding positive things to be thankful for and be aware of these, even if just for a short time, can be a boon for our mental health. We've been filling your mind with positive ideas about ourselves and our situation however, it becomes somewhat self-absorbed after some time. Try taking a more expansive view and be grateful for things previously not considered. Personally, it has brought me to becoming more aware of the natural world. When I am stuck in traffic, I can spot the flowers or plants through the windows of my stationary vehicle and I refocus on the beauty of it all. It is something else I was ignoring while surrounded by negative thoughts. From our health to relatives and friends, each of us has things about us that we ought to be grateful for . Training your mind to see the opportunities for gratitude could be the easiest way to lead an improved life. The the fact that we sleep under the protection of a roof and don't go to sleep hungry at least three times a week puts us in front of a large proportion of the population. Being grateful for the things we have is a sign of wealth itself.

Chapter 9: What is Emotional Intelligence?

The majority of business decisions that we make is in the context of our emotions. We base our decisions on how and what we feel. Research shows the emotional intelligence of people is two times higher likely to determine the success of your career than IQ. The IQ you have, is the criterion for you to be able to walk into the world of your job or your chosen profession. In reality, emotional intelligence is the key to the success and advancement. This is because all sorts of jobs involve directly or indirectly with others. Clearly human interactions and engagements are crucial in selling products, services and services as and selling ourselves.

They can be viewed as motivational systems - they can lead us to or away from something. In the midst of emotions are needs which can be met or not met.

For instance, if you enjoyed a food and it brought you a smile, that's an expression of emotion that indicates you've fulfilled a desire. Similar to that when the meal you enjoyed did not please your palate and made you feel like puking then you're likely to shout, smile, go away, or exhibit different emotions in expressing what you are feeling.

Another example is that generally when you're a cheerful person, you're likely to be social or social and maybe even more friendly. If you're depressed in contrast you're likely to be contemplative and logical, which could frequently bring down moody emotions.

The four components of emotional intelligence accomplish three things that are crucial:

Help inform our decisions

Help predict life outcomes

Help us learn about other people so that we can build healthy relationships.

In essence, emotional intelligence refers to the capacity to be aware of, manage and communicate one's feelings and emotions in a manner that improves relationships with others as well as efficient self-management. The ability to effectively manage your emotions is essential for both professional and personal achievement. This is due to the fact that the more you learn about and know yourself the more successful your professional and personal life will become.

"In an employment pool with high-IQ soft skills such as determination, drive, and discipline identify those who emerge as extraordinary."

Daniel Goleman

Inability to build your emotional intelligence could cause you to struggle in developing good relationships with your colleagues, friends, and business customers or colleagues. The development of your emotional intelligence will help you develop and sustain a variety of noncognitive skills that allow you to adjust to the demands of your life. As you increase your emotional intelligence, you'll be able to demonstrate these four essential abilities: self-awareness and the ability to manage yourself, social awareness and social abilities. In the various model that are used to describe Emotional Intelligence these skills can be described by:

Self-awareness: the ability to comprehend your emotions and feelings as well as the impact they have on your choices and actions. Therefore, this information is supposed to aid you in understanding your emotions and feelings in a manner that can help you make better decisions.

Social Awareness is the ability to comprehend the feelings, recognize and react to the feelings of others when you are in social settings.

Self-management, also known as self-care, is managing and controlling your feelings, emotions and desires. It also involves how you adjust to changing circumstances or situations.

Social skillsinclude the management of relationships, problem-solving abilities, and the capacity to influence, motivate and connect with others , as in addition to being able to handle conflict with prudence.

The model, which comes from Daniel Goleman's work includes a range of skills as well as knowledge, abilities, and behaviors that enhance leadership performance. All of which point to emotional intelligence.

You might want to learn more about The Emotional intelligence model, as well as the Trait Emotional Intelligence Model.

How can emotional intelligence assist transformation

It can be extremely difficult to get people to embrace change of any kind without doubt. Years of routine outcomes and deeply held beliefsprevent the majority of people away from accepting changes. Transformational leaders must realize that the change of thought and action require time and can't be made. Utilizing emotional intelligence, transformative leaders are able to think in accordance with team members' points of view. Consider exercising a lots of patience while building up capacity to ensure to ensure that the team is taught to recognize and participate in the necessity to changes.

Since emotional intelligence is already guiding on how to comprehend one's and other people's emotions and management, so leaders in transformation should not take criticisms, statements and body language as personal. There will be numerous occasions where these new leaders have to present new concepts or trigger times of tension that are essential for the growth and development of their teams However, they may be met with anger and apprehension by team members.

The most emotionally intelligent leaders understand the importance of growth to businesses and organisations and personal growth for individual team members . That's the reason why they are more concerned with helping individuals grow rather than being admired or appreciated, which is contrary to the traditional model of leadership. Instead of focusing on outcomes and performance always focusing on leaders who are transformational understand that in order to allow for truly transformative learning experiences to be successful, personal growth is more important than results in order to create an environment that encourages change.

Emotional Intelligence can aid in transformation through enabling leadership to create an environment that encourages change in the way they think, behave and act and the necessity of changing the way people interact and introduce fresh innovative ideas to the activities and thinking of team members, as well as the business and organizational settings in general.

Notes on the role of emotional intelligence in leadership transformation

It allows you to take control of the situation better. You are able to manage your emotions as well as understand the feelings of others more effectively.

Provides additional methods to effect change by creating a system of integration thoughts and feelings so that you can be aware of and control your the emotions of others and yourself and make informed decisions and manage your behaviors, and those of other people.

Because EI is a reference to the mental capabilities related to reacting to and processing emotions, which includes recognizing the expressions of emotions of other people as well as using emotions to boost thinking and controlling emotions to influence effective behavior Thus, these skills will likely to be linked to social competence adaptability to change, and overall organizational and personal achievement.

It helps shape and improve thoughts in ways that increase confidence and proficiency and reduces aggression, violence, and other behaviour problems. It can also help improve the ability to think critically, especially for younger and new transformative leaders.

Improving your emotional intelligence

Howard Gardner's Frames of Mind: The Theory of Multiple Intelligences, in 1983, introduced the concept that the conventional types of intelligence, like IQ do not completely explain cognitive abilities in his discussion of interpersonal intelligence (the capacity to recognize the motives, intentions and needs of others) and the ability to understand oneself (the capacity to know self-awareness as a means of understanding one's emotions as well as motivations, fears and anxieties).

Since the time, there have been a variety of writings on the idea of emotional intelligence. These include Daniel Goleman's bestseller, Emotional Intelligence: Why it is more important than IQ in 1995 which made the concept widely recognized.

While the idea of emotional intelligence has been subject to criticism for its impact on business and leadership Some researchers even saying that it's an inherent trait, others are of the opinion that it is possible to improve it through proper guidance and practice.

Therefore, in order to begin the path of increasing the emotional intelligence of your children, it's crucial to be able to tune into your emotions. While in some cases it may seem impossible, gaining the ability to listen to your own feelings is the initial and possibly most crucial step to take. It is also referred to as this the process self-awareness strategies.

It is essential for you to comprehend the reasons behind why you behave in certain ways or react to situations in certain ways. You should be able to recognize what you've done and why you've done it. Spend a few minutes during the day to think about "why did I behave in a certain way "Why do I feel this feeling? Analyze your choices, actions and reactions , and attempt to find answers within yourself. This will help you have a better understanding of your emotions, and being able to recognize these emotions like fear, anger or sadness or joy and so on, instead of trying to conceal them can help you improve managing your emotions. The most important aspect to increasing the emotional intelligence of your children is to make sure that your emotions and thoughts are in harmony.

Emotional intelligence is the capacity to see within and also the ability to reflect abilities to reflect on the present. This is crucial to discover your diverse personalities as well as beliefs and values.

It is not a good idea to dismiss or criticize your feelings until you have had the chance to process them. Be attentive to determine if you discover connections between your emotions and your thoughts, or in between the feelings you are experiencing and instances when you had similar experiences before. If you experience similar feelings and you are feeling overwhelmed, ask yourself "When did I experience this way previously?" When you do this, this will allow you to understand your feelings and emotions better.

If you're still not sure of your character traits It could be an excellent idea to find out more about it however, your natural tendencies and observation could suffice. As with most people, you'll already know if you're an extrovert or introvert highly judgmental or objective, highly sensitive or defensive. The more extrovert your personality is, the higher chances you have of handling your emotions and emotions as they are more likely for you to be socially vulnerable than an introvert. This knowledge can be an ideal starting point to fully understand what you're like and begin making adjustments and building upon your strengths.

If you know yourself well setting goals and achieving these goals becomes much easier since you know the person you truly are with what your weaknesses and strengths are, and the things your personality is capable of handling.

Connect to that energy in your subconscious thoughts and become more conscious of your unconscious thoughts and feelings. You can do this by permitting your thoughts to travel through your head without a care in which direction they take them. You can keep a record of your emotions that are weighing you down and also write down your thoughts in the morning, when you get up. Keep track of the dreams you have and note how your feel when you wake up and note any dreams that are recurring which could be a result of a certain pattern in your thinking system. Additionally, regular writing about your ideas and feelings will assist you in developing more self-awareness.

Learning styles are vital to growth and development. As an effective leader, being open to new knowledge is crucial for achieving success. Finding your preferred learning style not only increases your personal development and ability, but also helps you to perform at the highest level as well as increase your self-awareness. The three primary types of learning are the auditory, visual and the kinaesthetic. It is essential to determine the one that best suits you and to know where you fit for learning that is effective to take place.

Chapter 10: Teach Your Children to recognize their emotional intelligence

EMOTIONAL Intelligence CHILDREN

Emotional Intelligence must also be built within your kids. This helps them to be more competent to succeed in whatever profession they choose to pursue once they are adults.

Children with a good EQ will be able to be able to understand and respond to the feelings of others which means they have a variety of skills that are common. If your child is able to recognize emotions and utilize it in a way that is appropriate, he will likely possess exceptional interpersonal abilities. This skill will bring him just a little closer to his goals and goals.

The growth of your kid begins when they reach the age of three. This is the perfect time to assist to develop his emotional intelligence, too. How can you help your child build his emotional intelligence?

Take note of your child's behavior, how react to certain situations? Are they able to manage his emotions or does he has difficulty solving issues? If he's unable to be compassionate to other people, is impulsive and teachers are unhappy with his behavior and behavior, then he needs to improve an emotional intelligence.

It is important to be aware that the EQ of your child's can be improved with your direction. The factors that determine how your child's ability to cope with the demands of life depend not just on his academic abilities. They must possess personality traits like patience, flexibility, and self-control to overcome the challenges of life successfully. This can lead to an optimistic relationship with people.

Here are some suggestions to boost the emotional development of your children's

Inspire safe attachment.

Be attentive to your child's needs to encourage their intellectual and emotional development. This will promote a safe bond and form the foundation for his development of EQ and, eventually his social capabilities.

Aid your child to monitor his own behavior.

Aid them in understanding their feelings. It is possible to do this by talking with children about the way that a specific event can trigger them to react in a specific manner. Talk about anger, jealousy or jealousy and discuss it in the most simple manner you can. Recognizing the emotions will give children a greater chances of responding correctly to them.

Aid them in self-regulation.

Aid them in learning self-regulation by showing them how to be able to avoid stressful situations. This can be achieved by engaging in recreational activities. Each time they conquer the challenge do not forget to congratulate them for their efforts.

Improve their communication abilities.

Aid them in enhancing their communication capabilities. You can do this by playing entertaining games. Instruct the child to engage in conversation and explore diverse subjects. Ask questions that are difficult and observe what the child's response is. Discuss different scenarios in school and how the child is feeling during these situations.

Make sure you have some problem-solving sessions with your children.

Encourage your children to solve issues by offering ideas on how to find the best solution. You can also try brainstorming with them, so that they can be motivated to share their ideas.

Be open to their emotional and their responses.

Accept that they can be upset at times. Do not scold them for it. Instead, tell them that their reaction is normal, and then teach them to deal with the reactions.

Help them to recognize the emotions of other people.

This can be accomplished by asking them what they feel about someone else and how they can respond to it.

Find other ways to express their anger.

Help them realize that in difficult situations, it's not always wise to punish people. You can use a different approach instead. Demonstrate what those strategies might be, such as paying attention to playtime as well as counting to ten and taking deep breaths.

Find out what drives them to be at their best.

If you do this you'll learn to further motivate them and improve their EQ.

It's Possible to improve your emotional intelligence?

Do you think your EQ improve? When dealing with others, whether in the workplace, at school and even relationships it's crucial to be equipped with an adequate degree of emotional intelligence. You could attend some training seminars to increase your EQ however, can you be sure that there is a 100 percent guarantee that it will actually increase? While IQ is not a measurable thing, EQ can. Practice often until you reach the level of intelligence that can benefit you in your daily interactions.

Here are some things to take into you should take into consideration when trying to improve your EQ

The EQ level EQ is small but not stiff.

The ability to identify and manage your emotions is relatively stable for a long time. It is affected by your genes and past experiences. However, that doesn't mean that you can't modify it in any way. Actually, improvement is feasible with the help of persistence and supervision. The only problem is how willing they are to give it a shot.

The best training programs are there to benefit you.

It isn't impossible to boost your EQ Many training programs are conducting seminars and training on methods to improve. It is just a matter of choose wisely the one that is right for you. The most crucial thing to take into consideration when choosing an program is the trust you have in the coach or speaker. You must be able to trust that he can work miracles to boost your in terms of your EQ.

Improved performance through specific feedback

A lot of times you don't know how other people view your character. You might not think that you're nice, but imagine that others also think that way, creating an EQ that is low. There are people who think that they are very confident and excellent, so they live by their image, but they don't realize that it's the reverse.

Certain coaches and methods are superior to other techniques and coaches.

It is always recommended to research the training programs before deciding to join one. This way, you'll be able to select wisely which one will fit you the best.

Some people are more easy to coach than others.

There are instances when those who are the most patient, or most skilled coach or speaker is not able to succeed in increasing the EQ of a person. This is due to the fact that every person is at a different stage of being able to catch up. Some might catch up quick, but others might take longer to get better.

Chapter 11: Working On Emotional Intelligence

The concept of emotional intelligence is believed to exist in four main aspects - self-awareness and empathy, self-management, and social awareness as well as interpersonal relationships abilities.

Let's look at each one to find some suggestions about how you can tackle these.

Self-Awareness is the ability to recognize and comprehend our own emotions as well as the effect they can have on our relationships and self-esteem.

Are you aware of your personality? What are your dreams and goals?

Request feedback from others on the strengths you have and your weaknesses. Ask them and how people would define you, and what their opinions on what your goals or interests are. If you find this too intimidating you can take online personality tests. You can also make a the list of traits that are frequently used.

Make a few moments each day to write down your reflections at the start or at the end of your day. If you have trouble writing make a video of a minute on your smartphone and then review the day later.

It is a good idea to think about what's most important to you and then writing down a list of goals or plans can help you build the self-confidence. You'll be surprised by how much everyone is trying to learn new skills and saving up to purchase something, improving your body, improving relations with your family or friends, planning an active retirement, or studying more or anything else.

Once we've got a sense of who we are , we begin to consider how we can handle our own interactions and those of other people.

Self-management strategies are your personal arsenal of tools to aid you in developing a program and regulate your emotional reactions and impulses that can lead your course off.

The benefit of having a plan is that it provides an objective point of view and allows you to prioritize tasks and make sure that you don't let basic self-care activities like fitness or time for relaxation slip off your radar. Start with the most challenging tasks and keep working on them consistently until they become a habit.

Self-management for emotional issues involves focusing on your attitude, managing your feelings and building confidence. Spending some time with your own self by creating an early-morning routine is a method to boost your confidence and assist you in completing your self-care routine right from the start. Exercise, journaling, meditation and repeating your morning affirmations are all great options.

Mindfulness can be a wonderful method to allow yourself some space to process your emotions . It can be as long or short as you'd like.

The five senses mindfulness method can help reduce stress. It is a great option when you are in a short supply, or to take a short refresher during hectic days.

Five Senses Technique Five Senses Technique

Find an indoor or outdoor place where you can relax in a comfortable position for a few minutes. It is best to devote around. 30 seconds per sense.

Shut your eyes, and begin to pay attention to your breathing. Relax for a few minutes and, when you feel relaxed, begin to listen , and be aware of what you detect. Try to focus on the most distant sounds to see the sounds that you can hear beyond.

Then, pay attention to the smell you detect. It may not be an identifiable scent but it could be something like smokey, fresh, or the scent of food, or perfume.

Spend about. 30 seconds here, and then start moving your mouth as you contemplate what you might smell. This could refer to the leftovers of your last drink , or food items you've eaten. It could be a feeling of bitterness or sweetness.

We'll now move to the touch. While they are still in motion, observe that your fingers are as they rest upon your knees, or on your lap. Be aware of the texture of your clothing against your skin, and feel the cushion of your floor or seat beneath your feet. If you're outside you might feel the breeze blowing around you the breeze or the warmth of the sun.

Open your eyes, then take a look around. Select an object that you want to focus on and absorb everything about it's appearance. Are you able to tell if it is moving or stationary? Its colour depth and size. Are they transparent or opaque?

What materials are they composed of? Are they plain or patterned?

Bring your attention back to your breath , and then do an easy stretch.

How are you feeling?

The aim of this practice is to give your mind and body to relax and focus on paying attention to each of your senses. This is a wonderful method to manage your self and the goal behind this being to stop yourself from reaching the point of being overwhelmed. Be on top of it and reap the rewards of more focus, improved ability to manage stress and more productive ability.

Chapter 12: Feelings are An Answer To Your Interpretation Of Information . Interpretations can be altered

As I mentioned earlier When we feel unhappy, angry or even joyous We usually connect this emotion to some event. I remember the first time I had a baby. It was a wonderful experience, I felt happy, full of affection and love for this precious baby. I was in a state of bliss for months. I truly believed that I was fortunate and blessed.

At the at the same time, an neighbor and acquaintance of mine had a baby as well. She was awestruck by the huge burden and changes this new life was set to bring about and she began to feel depressed and isolated. Then she received a diagnosis of postnatal depression, and provided with the needed assistance. Another example of two similar events, but with a different emotional response.

The same experience may trigger different emotions based on the interpretation we make of the event

It's crucial to remember in this moment that there's an absolute right and wrong reaction. It's just our internal direction that tells us what we're feeling. For managers or leaders it is not your job to make someone build emotional intelligence, or evaluate them for having emotions that are negative or even judge the reaction or assumption. It is up to you to comprehend the process your team members are going through and accept that all people are different, and providing the proper amount of encouragement.

My 14-year-old son was involved in a crash. He was injured, but not too badly. He was on the school bus but did not notice the vehicle. The car was badly damaged , and the driver got shaken. I was very concerned about the driver. I tried to remind officers that this was not the driver's fault. My son was severely bruised. He went on a few trips into the hospital. However, he miraculously he had no severe injuries.

After that, I received an email from the wife of the driver threatning me with legal action if I didn't pay for the damages to the vehicle. My initial reaction was anger and a feeling of injustice. I was furious at a time when I wanted to not point fingers of blame at the driver that he was turning the tables and tried to claim the damages I incurred. For the first 10 minutes I was lost in my negative feelings. Then I realized the mistake I had made as I was trying to focus on the incident. I had been generous in my effort to ensure that the driver was safe This was the way I was rewarded!

You can interpret situations and events in your life the way you'd prefer.

I stopped for a moment and realized the fact that my reaction was based on an perception of the situation rather than the incident itself. I immediately calmed myself as I began thinking critically about the incident. I realized that the driver's actions were not related to me. He was free to take whatever action he deemed was right and I had to trust that things would go as planned. I was able immediately to shift my perspective and consequently my feelings about the incident changed as well.

It's true that the majority of people base their decisions on their feelings about something. Sometimes, this could have devastating results if there's no mental reasoning that is behind the emotion. Some crimes and revenge are committed due to the emotions people experience.

Psychologically speaking, we fall into two camps psychologically. Carl Jung's work "psychological types" was recognized through the work of Myers and Briggs the mother and daughter team that invented their Myers Briggs Type indicator tool. In Jung's research He identifies two fundamentally opposing ways that we make decisions. We make choices in response to our feelings about something or make choices based on what we think about something.

Also, we use different decision making styles at different times and in various circumstances. Nobody makes decisions solely through feelings, or even thinking. We just have a tendency to follow a method that feels more comfortable to us.

I'm mostly a feeler decision maker. When I got the letter regarding my son's accident, I was able to feel my feelings first , before I could be conscious about the content in the document.

Once I was calmed and began to think more rationally , I realized that I was able to respond in many different ways. And I was able to interpret data in a way that my system of guidance told me was not positive or choose an interpretation that produced an entirely different emotional impact. My job in this situation, was to pick the thought that resonated with me and helped me feel emotionally secure again.

Is this a sign that those who make decisions from a place of thinking are in better shape? It is possible, but at other times, they make choices without realizing, or even ignoring, their own emotional guidance system in the first place. The emotional response can occur in later.

We all feel at initially, but then we become conscious of our thoughts, and others think initially, before becoming conscious of our emotions

I've witnessed more conflicts occur in the workplace due to certain people prefer to live their lives rationally by thinking things through and applying their knowledge to facts, whereas certain people use their emotions and their feelings to gauge the things they enjoy, dislike, their relationship to others , and the way they make their decisions. The difference between feeling and thinking when not understood and respected can create chaos.

A few of you might have seen an article entitled "Men come from Mars and women come from Venus" written by John Gray. The book is designed to improve men and women in their relationships by studying the various methods "Thinkers as well as Feelers" connect". It's a bit stereotyped because it assumes that men are thinkers , and women are people who feel. This isn't always the case, as you are aware.

Today, we can all utilize both the mind and the body to make decisions, we generally prefer one way or the other. As we grow older and become more experienced, we tend to adjust our preferred approach, and keeping our fingers crossed, we end up being quite well-balanced.

To be clear. Our emotions are determined by our thoughts about something. We are able to absorb information, go through it, and we take the information and interpret it. Based on our interpretation, whether it is negative or positive will determine what we think about it. The majority of our thinking is quick and/or inconspicuous that we do not know what is causing us to feel the way we do. For people who have an interest in thinking, thought process is the first priority. For those with a sense preference, feelings are the first.

A high level of emotional intelligence is the ability to make decisions with the heart.

Many people discuss taking decisions from their heart. This is often interpreted as making decisions based on how we feel. However, I believe decision-making from the heart is taken when our thoughts and emotions are in sync, the alignment is in tune with our inner self and we are feeling positive. In other words your thoughts regarding the person, event or circumstance are aligned with your own natural state of peace, happiness and forgiveness. Your emotions reflect that. You feel calm and content.

The fact that our emotions act as an indicator system that lets us know if our thoughts are in line with our real happiness is extremely valuable information. If we experience a lot of negative emotions, then we've got the key to unlock the way to happiness. The old saying says, "you can lead a horse to the water however you won't be able to let it drink".

Do you want to feel right? Or do you wish to be content? It's a decision

There will be a large number of people who don't consider that our emotions are not an acceptable response or call to action, so it is impossible to progress without them making the most important decision we all take at some stage. This is Are you looking the right thing? Or do you wish to be content? Thinking in different ways to be content is the path less traveled. That brings to the next tip that reacting could result in the same outcomes, pause lets you decide on your answer.

Chapter 13: Triggers of Emotion

We have seen the different types of emotions and the way they function against one another in the things we do. What is the cause of these feelings? Do they come out independently? No! Every emotion is the result of certain stimuli or arousals that we refer to as emotional Triggers. We react positively or negatively to certain triggers of emotion at times. Cool colors, a attractive appearance, pleasant smell can bring us a positive feeling known as happiness. However, an unsettling color or smell, or a sour appearance can trigger negative emotions such as disgust or anger.

There are times when we choose something to purchase and then go to the shop, but feel something different than the one we imagined in mind, and we rethink our choices. We might have been enticed by the brand's new color or advertising message, packaging or whatever the reason. Something has caused us to take a choice (emotional output) toward a specific brand's name, product or image.

The reason why these emotional triggers are crucial for firms?

There are a variety of benefits these feelings bring for a company and handful of them are

* If a client is motivated by a positive feeling, they continue to seek out that satisfaction with the business. For us it's an instance of MARKETING CONTENT.

When a customer experiences the emotion, he immediately recalls your company (content or speech) which brought him to the similar state of mind prior to, which boosts the loyalty of your customers.

Most of the time, it causes to an impulse purchase

It is obvious that it is emotional triggers that drive customers to take an step, which could be purchasing or eating in the context of marketing.

Different types of Triggers

Marketing psychologists classify these triggers into two kinds in accordance with their characteristics, presence and the manner in which they guide us to take act.

External Triggers are the specific information that tell us on what to do next. They are present in our every day offline or online travels. E.g. Signboards for outdoor billboards and Signal Lamps and Call-For-Action buttons that are on websites, etc.

Internal Triggers

The decision-making process for the next step is provided by an association that is stored with the user's memories. Typically, marketers tackle this with well-thought-out campaigns, which trigger our emotions and behave as they planned. E.g. raising awareness of the importance of wearing helmets by imagining the tragic deaths that have caused by the lack of helmets.

Let's look at how these triggers could be constructed in a manner to be incorporated into our everyday marketing campaigns.

Chapter 14: Identifying Your Emotions and The Emotions of Others

It's crucial to know the emotions you're experiencing prior to trying to determine the emotions of someone else. In the end, if you don't have the ability to ride a bicycle and you don't know how to help someone else learn the skill of riding it. If you don't have knowledge of yourself, you won't be able to be aware of the knowledge of other people.

Understanding Your Emotions

There are eight essential steps to learn to recognize your emotions Although certain of them may appear to be insignificant or irrelevant, you should move beyond your initial doubts and test them.

1. Take a look at the physical reaction you have to an event.

One of the primary indicators an individual is the physical manifestation of the emotion. It may be different for you than for me, however there's almost always an emotional response that is associated with the feeling. Be aware of your body's signals. For certain people, anxiety and anxiety may manifest as tension in the chest or tight shoulders. Betrayal, sadness, grief and distrust may all manifest as stomach pain or tension in the abdominal region. The flushing may occur on facial, ear or chest.

The feeling of happiness can manifest as feeling lighter physically, or it may cause flushing of the forehead or cheeks. It could feel like a tingling in your feet, hands or even the head.

#2 Determine the emotion that you're feeling.

It's important to remain absolutely clean when dealing with the emotions you feel and trying to understand them. Therefore, be sure to remain alcohol - and drug-free while you're implementing these techniques. Many people resort to drugs to record their reactions to their emotions, however one of the best ways to determine what they're and how to deal with the emotions is by feeling the emotions. When you are in a secure place where you can feel the emotions in your body, allow them to run go and consult this chart to determine the emotions you may be experiencing.

#3 Don't make a mistake.

One of the main reasons people avoid their feelings or get better in ignoring them is that they judge their feelings. For instance, if someone close to you passes away then you could say to yourself that your grief will pass with time and the world moves on which is what you should do. You could tell yourself that it's foolish to be angry and you'll never be in the future.

If you keep these intense emotions and don't allow them to be experienced in a rational and calm way, you could feel like you're screaming irrationally at the smallest of things.

4. Make time for yourself.

It's very easy for us to forget about our feelings because we lead such busy lives, and we move from one thing to the next, and one thinking to the following. Spend a few minutes to reflect or be with yourself after an event to observe what transpires. Be present and attentive is something that you need to strive to improve at all times and can help you understand what you can learn after a few minutes of thinking about what you're feeling.

One of the primary ways that people can are able to escape their feelings is to make use of technology or work on an additional task. When you're not happy with your feelings, make sure that you're not utilizing something other than technology, food or cleaning chores etc.--to take your mind off of what's happening.

#5 Note it down.

Writing is among the least understood types of therapy. Many people aren't aware that writing down the emotions they're feeling is an excellent way to recognize their feelings and discover ways to manage their feelings later on. Spend a few minutes to record what you're feeling. Once you're more relaxed you can revisit the experience and look at ways to manage your emotions better at some point in the near future.

#6 Talk with someone who's understanding.

As difficult as it may seem, it's crucial to allow others into your life. It's not a vulnerability; it requires the courage to open up with someone about how you really feel. In addition, you'll be able to improve how to listen by listening to what they've got to say to you later. They may offer some helpful suggestions on how to handle your emotions and also the circumstances which led them to their conclusions.

If there's not a person in your home or with a family member who you can talk to, talk to someone online or over the phone. There are hotlines to those feeling alone, and contrary to common belief, those on the other side really take note of how you're experiencing. The reason they're in this situation in the first place if they didn't.

7 Listen to some tunes.

Music triggers emotion in people of all ages. In spite of trying to get rid of whatever you're feeling; one song could be a thumping blast and instantly trigger emotions that you didn't realize you felt. If you're looking to tap into a particular emotion, select a tune music that evokes that emotion inside the person you are.

#8 Take time to do a daily reflection.

After a long day, it is recommended to spend a few minutes before retiring to think about the events that occurred through the entire day. What caused you to feel depressed, angry, sad or even elated? Keep a notebook at night so that you can record the emotions you felt; this way, you're completing steps five and eight simultaneously! Reflect on how you could handle those circumstances and feelings differently if they had been negative. Then think about how peaceful, joyful or even joyful feelings at specific times during the day.

Believing in the Emotions of Others

Three ways that you can gauge the emotion of another such as looking at their body language or listening to your instincts and analyzing their energy.

Watching Body Language

It's well-known that words comprise only 7 percent of the way people communicate; however the body language we use accounts for 55 percent of our communication, while our voice tone accounts for the remaining 30 percent. Don't get too naive about body language signals since we all live in different settings and the same body language signal can be used to express many different feelings.

Here are some illustrations of the body language clues.

Be aware of the person's appearance. If you're reading someone else's profile take note of whether they're wearing business clothing such as jeans, a t-shirt and jeans or tight clothing designed to be attractive or religious symbols which indicate religious dedication. A person who has arms crossed in business clothes might be trying to convince that they are dominant, whereas people with their arms crossed while wearing jeans and a t-shirt could be being defensive, which is two distinct emotions.

Take note of the other person's posture. When you're observing the posture of someone else check if they're putting their heads up (confidence) as well as if they're moving hesitantly (low confidence in themselves). Are they showing off (egotistical)?

Be aware of the physical movements of the person you are watching. Are they leaning, but away from you? Examine the places the areas where they're taking their learning. A person generally leans towards someone they love and away from those they do not like. Are they sitting in a slouche position with their arms or legs crossed? A person who is in this position may be angry, defensive or trying to protect themselves. If you see someone crossing your legs they are likely to point their toes towards the person they feel most comfortable around. When they're hiding hands like on their laps or in their pockets or even putting them behind their backs or behind their backs, they're trying to relax themselves when in a awkward situation or feel pressured. A person who bites their lips might require self-soothing in times of stress.

Learn to interpret the facial expressions. The expressions of emotions can be evident on certain faces, however they could be more difficult to discern on the other person. A deep frown suggests that the person is worried or overthinking an issue. The feet of a crowd suggest that someone is laughing frequently. Lips that are purred can indicate an expression of anger, contempt or even bitterness. A jaw that is clenched and grinds teeth may indicate being tense.

Pay attention to your intuition

You can be able to sense the emotions of another person beyond their body language and words. Your intuition is what your body is telling you rather than what your brain is telling you. It's nonverbal communication that is not obvious, but your eyes, ears and even your touch take in these subtle clues and create an impression that you form in your mind. If you are trying to comprehend someone else, what matters is the personality of the person and not the external signals they display. Intuition lets you perceive more and provide an improved picture of the individual.

Be true to your intuition. Pay attention to what your gut telling you, particularly the first time you meet people. It's an instinctual reaction that occurs before you have an opportunity to think about the person. It reveals whether you're at ease or not. The gut feelings can be felt quickly as part of primitive reactions. They're your primal, internal brain transmitting information to you.

Feel the goosebumps. Feel the tingling sensations you feel when you get to meet someone new: they could be positive or negative. They could happen while you're with someone who you love having time with. Or could happen when you're with those who give you creeps. Pay attention to them. They're usually right.

Take note of glimpses of understanding. When you are talking you may get an epiphany regarding a person quickly. Be aware of these. If you don't, you might overlook these. People tend to move on to the next thought at such a rapid pace that the most important insights are overlooked.

Be aware of your instinctual empathy. Sometimes, you may notice the physical signs and feelings in your body. This is a type of empathy. If you're reading another person's words, ask yourself whether you're feeling exactly the same emotions they're experiencing.

Understanding the Emotional Energy of Others

Expressions of emotions are a powerful representation of our energy or the energy we're giving off. We can detect these through our senses. Certain people are happy to be around as they enhance our mood and boost our energy. Some people feel drained and instinctively would like to escape them. This energy is present when we're close to one another but it's not evident.

Feel the presence of another. This is the vibe you'd like to convey and is not required to be in sync with your actions and words. It's the mood that surrounds us. When you read about someone else take note of whether they've an inviting presence that makes you want be around them. Or are they making you feel uncomfortable and feel like you'd prefer to stay removed from the person?

Pay attention to the eyes of the person you are watching. Eyes transmit powerful signals to others. As the brain also has the ability to transmit electromagnetic signals, research have revealed that the eyes transmit what we're feeling more than any other. Be sure to look at your eyes. Are they happy or peaceful? Are they sexy, romantic or angry, mean or depressed? Find out if they're trying to cover up their feelings by avoiding your gaze.

Consider the way someone feels when you hug them or handshake or feel them. People exchange their emotions through physical contact, much like the electrical energy. Check whether a handshake or hug from another person is warm, confident, and at ease. Does it make you feel uncomfortable because it's cold, clammy or sluggish?

Pay attention to the voice tone or laughter. It is possible to tell something about someone when they smile. When reading someone's text pay attention to the way their voice affects your. Consider whether their laughter is genuine or is harsh. Do their manner of speaking suggest that they are interested? Or is it just a way to please you to escape the circumstance?

The ability to read others can be helpful in your business and personal life. Being able to read a person's feelings and to understand their motives can make the difference between making a sale and signing an agreement with a client or client. It could be the difference between a caring and loving relationship or one that is quickly dissolved.

Once you've figured out the concept of emotional intelligence it's components, and how to discern emotions, let's consider the ways to make tiny changes over the time of the month to become emotionally smart.

Chapter 15: Building on Self-Confidence

There is a lot of talk about confident people all over the world but it's something difficult to achieve in your own life. Everyone has experienced or is likely to feel in the beginning of their life a lack of self-confidence throughout their lives. Self-confidence is a challenge to develop, particularly in the vulnerable period of adolescence and childhood in which the person is exposed to a variety of negativity, no matter if it's from their friends and family, media or the Internet hormones, etc. We all were born without self-doubt; we didn't have to be weighed down by thoughts of whether or not we were worthy or if we were smart enough, if we properly dressed, whether we would fit in or not, etc. The moment we realized that we were not ourselves and our own shortcomings, or the time we began going to school and encountered the wrath of a child that was brutally honest or perhaps a teacher who was strict and we felt our self-confidence shattering.

Self-esteem problems usually have their roots in childhood traumas, experiences or separations of parents and friends, or even physical or sexual assault. It's a complex and delicate issue. Self-esteem sufferers view the world as hostile and think of themselves as victimized. This usually creates a feeling of powerlessness. Most people who have confidence issues have a tough to express their feelings. They're afraid of experiencing situations in their lives, and believe that they're not enough or do not deserve the things they have.

If you're able to be a victim of these sentiments and are aware that you're not confident in yourself then congratulations ... that means you're conscious of your feelings and the setbacks. Self-confidence can be built gradually and slowly. Just like everybody else can attain it through perseverance and specific actions.

There are a few actions that will help you improve your self-confidence and place yourself in a more positive mood and state of mind, to feel confident in your skin. Maybe you've already learned the basics, or maybe you're already practicing these, but let's take a the time to look over each step separately.

1. Be aware of yourself. We all believe that we are completely aware of ourselves However, you'll be shocked to discover that very few people even know who they are. One of the most gruesome things is that a lot individuals are their self-defeating adversaries (negative comments, negative talk and self-doubt, negative thinking as well as.). The best way to take on your adversaries is to learn about it completely.

How do you identify yourself? Simple , observe and observe your thoughts. It is possible to take notes and examine the reasons you think negative thoughts, and whether you really believe in them. It's not difficult to be a victim of self-deflection particularly when you've been doing this for a lengthy period of time. But, in order to achieve an equilibrium, you need to think of your strengths and weaknesses. What are you able to do well? What are your most effective qualities and achievements ... you can see that there ought to be at the very least one! Consider your weaknesses (your limitative beliefs) and examine if they're actually limitations or thought up as a result of your long-term focus on factors that are holding you back. Don't be afraid of diving deep into your brain. Be aware of it all be aware of it, acknowledge it and then comprehend it.

2. Stand tall . Posture does it's magic, even when you don't feel like you're in the best shape of your life. If you find yourself not standing up straight, make a conscious effort to stand taller. Standing with your back straight and your head slightly elevated will not just give you a great impression of yourself, but it will assist you in presenting yourself as someone with confidence in your self. Practice this for a

while and notice what people think to you, how they perceive your face and how they talk about you when you're in a good posture. You'll be surprised!

3. Set goals - Begin by attempting something small, just as an experiment. Don't abandon the idea until you've achieved it. Achieving your goals will result in a multitude of positive feelings and you'll be happy with your accomplishments. The pleasant feelings can be a great stimulant that builds confidence in yourself and gives you the feeling confident and competent to achieve your objectives.

4. Be grateful and give thanks This is the way to go regardless of the circumstances, since counting your blessings awakens an awareness level where you are aware of the privilege you have compared to other people. Be grateful that you woke up today and you had food on the table. Thank God for the bills you need to pay since it means you are employed and have money. Be thankful for those in your life

who are there for you regardless of the circumstances. Be grateful for things that ease your life like your computer or the Internet phones, books and so on.

5. Stop putting off a task - The numbing feeling that you get whenever you delay something to the future can create anxiety. Instead of putting off work until next week or tomorrow take it on now and finish it. You'll feel fulfilled, happy and lighter. Your future self tomorrow or next week will be grateful.

6. Exercise - You're aware of the many benefits from exercising. Your body will be more toned and dopamine levels rise, which will make you feel more relaxed.

7. Don't forget to smile . If you take life too seriously, it can be difficult therefore don't forget to smile. Smile at people or at your children, or at you in your mirror... The idea might seem absurd, but a simple smile is sure to help you feel better. Imagine that your winning the lottery. What do you think you'd look like? Do you

remember the many times that you were approached by someone who smiled and you responded with a smile, being happy for no specific reason. What better way to be that first to smile? It's absolutely free and easy to relax and creates a great mood.

8. Be hydrated and taking good care of yourself is an ideal idea. Drinking plenty of water helps keep your cells hydrated and thus helps them recover. When your body is healthy and healthy, there's no reason to experience any negative feelings. People who aren't well-hydrated tend to be more stressed, angry, depressed as well as slow and inactive. Make sure you drink drinking eight glasses of fluids each day.

9. Be able to sleep enough and always tired will not do you anything positive. The fact that you are reducing your sleep time so that you can stare at your computer or phone or anything else you might do in the absence of sleep is likely to damage your immune system and impact your day-to-day life. When you're getting enough sleep

you will not only see your body recover and be refreshed, but you'll also be able to complete your tasks throughout the day.

10. Get rid of old habits. Start with a small step. For example, instead of going to the office by bus, you could try walking or biking (if your work isn't too far away). You could start your day 10 minutes earlier, or drink the or tea rather than coffee. Small adjustments will provide your brain with the knowledge to think that it's doing something different or something that isn't in your normal routine. Be sure to stick to the new habits and observe how they impact your life. It's been proven that even small modifications can alter old habits and create positive emotions. Start small and the impact can be enormous.

11. Wear nice clothes Dress nice - You don't need to purchase new clothes to wear this. It's enough to wear your favourite dress or shirt, or even something you don't often wear but you love. Wearing clothes you love can enhance your mood, and you'll be amazed at how

many people praise on you or even look at you in a different way.

12. Declutter - Take away everything you don't need; throw away everything you don't need and have accumulated dust. Donate away your clothes that you don't wear. By getting rid of things that are no longer needed and making room for new items. This will give you a sense in control of your lifestyle and you'll be able to clean your home while doing it.

13. Don't think about negative thoughts anymore. Like you toss away everything that is no longer of use to you and do the same thing with the negative thoughts creating a negative impact on your life. Imagine placing all your thoughts into a bag before throwing it away. This isn't something you'll do just one time and expect to observe change. If you notice a wave of negative thoughts forming into your mind, you can open the bag, take the thoughts, then discard them. If you are confronted by a negative thought then tell

yourself "It's simply a negative thought" and decide not to respond to it.

14. Enjoy time spent with those who make you feel happy and motivate you to become better . Simple as that. Contact your friends that inspire you and invite them to drinks. Call your grandparents or parents and share a meal with them. Ask their opinions and tell them about your plans. Note how relaxed, comfortable and happy you are.

15. Make sure you do more of what makes you feel happy Do not ignore things that bring you joy because you're busy or because your family or spouses aren't around or you simply don't like it. You want to watch the film but nobody else is able to take you to the theater? Buy an admission ticket, purchase popcorn and then enjoy the movie all by yourself. Go fishing or read a book, write a novel, go to the latest play ... Simply take at least 2 hours per week doing something that you love even if that means doing it by

yourself. This will help you become more self-sufficient.

Chapter 16: Strategies to Inspire Interest

You now have the fundamental steps to follow to be an improved listener. What can you do to apply this to your professional life? Maybe you don't have any partner you'd like to build a stronger intimacy. Perhaps you're one of the people who are driven and focused on their careers around the world, and you want people to stop believing that you don't value their opinions. Perhaps you're required to be perceived as a more team player. How can listening help get you on the right track towards a more rewarding and prosperous business career?

Simply.

More than ever before, listening is essential in business and this is due to the fact that the people are overwhelmed by the technological boom. With more texting and emails and texting, the art of having an enjoyable face-to-face conversation is being ruined by people who are constantly checking their emails and snooping over messages. Meetings are getting more sought-after and this means having small rooms filled with a crowd of males who talk about topics that may not interest you or be of any interest to you however, paying attention is noticed.

Here are some strategies you can use active listening in order to propel your career to a whole new level of achievement:

I. Active Listening:

If it's bosses there's nothing they love greater than the knowledge that directives they're granting and the jobs they're tasked with are done by employees who are completely committed, completely understanding and part of their team. When you sit and silently nod it doesn't mean anything in the eyes of your employer. Participate in the conversation.

Ask questions, speak up and let everyone know that you're there and demonstrate your commitment to the job in front of you. Your boss will be impressed by your enthusiasm and passion. Do not ask questions that aren't relevant but. Make sure you ask questions that help you gain a better understanding or allow you to complete your task more efficiently. This is called active listening. Let your boss know that you're interested.

II. Stop, collaborate and Listen:

Vanilla Ice has it right. In the case of your colleagues, don't look to be the most dominant, but try to be successful. When you listen to the thoughts and opinions of your colleagues in projects, without the goal of changing their views to your goals They will feel more connected to you. This will not only provide you with the advantage of understanding your coworkers in the same place, who's as committed in the same way as you, and has the most innovative idea, but it will also increase the bond between you and the people who you collaborate with. A network of peers is beneficial, particularly as you advance within your professional lives. Make sure you have that enthusiasm and a sense of community between your colleagues and you.

III. It's not my job. I'm an asset

There's a difference between an employee and asset. Are you aware of the distinction? Employees are disposable. Employees can be replaced. Remember the art of mouth, mind, and ears? The ear feeds the mind , and this results in knowledge. This leads to power. Did you know that the saying goes: Knowledge is power? That's certainly also true. If you're looking to improve your knowledge to become more valuable and be a valuable asset, begin listening and taking in all the information you can. This will demonstrate to your boss that you're aware of the ropes, that you're committed to your business, and you're prepared to take the necessary steps to continue pushing forward. This is how you'll set yourself apart from your colleagues.

IV. the Power of Three:

Okay, now that you've felt the power and the foundation of each of them add them together and see what happens. Not just will your boss feel confident in you and, if you complete your work perfectly it will; But your colleagues will also be inspired by you as they will feel appreciated because of your willingness to listen to their thoughts, and you'll be an essential resource for the company. All of this will be put together to create a strong impact. If you follow through and excel with all of your tasks that you can be unstoppable, and be considered to be the ultimate team player. Achieving one of these goals will make your life easier and combining all three will make your career extremely prosperous.

Do not expect instant results, but be aware of the changes in your behavior with each conversation. When you interact with many more people, and are fully conversing with them, be it your boss or coworkers will notice shifts in the way they behave in relation to you. Therefore, start making changes starting on Monday. Your professional life should be something that is truly devoted and attractive and others will notice.

Chapter 17: Controlling Your Thoughts

Mind is the primary source of all power for every human being and you must be in control of it, and not vice versa. Two of the lessons are focused on emotions that are already present. That's the reason why the third lesson is for you. Lesson 3, you will be taught to manage you thoughts prior to it is able to stir emotions within your.

Every thought triggers emotions. If you are thinking or recollecting thoughts, you expose yourself to the feelings that is associated with it. However, most people are unable to make their minds not think. It's a natural part of the process and, regardless of whether you like the idea or not particularly at times of sudden change it can remind you of the time you were there and suddenly when you're in the middle of the conversation to your manager, you're frustrated or lonely. In this scenario you don't have time to perform a self-check before the meeting because you're already engulfed into a social encounter.

Exercise 3

There are two options for managing your thoughts. One is meditation and the other is conditioning.

Meditation

Meditation is a way to manage your thoughts. It is to remove your mind from it. Consider it to be merely clouds that are passing through. Take a look without judgement, and the emotions that accompany them won't bubble onto the surface.

Meditation does not need to be conducted in a formal manner in which you lie on your back and say "ohm". The practice can be performed any time and anywhere. It can happen in the middle of a tranquil walk along the park or along the beach at night, in traffic, on the way between work and home, or at home. The most important thing to remember when doing contemplation is the fact that it has to be performed in solitude and in a tranquil space.

When you sit down to meditate you want to be objective instead of being judgmental. Being critical means being curious. It is important to ask questions, do not presume to know the answer. This is how you train the mind to differentiate your mind from your self. They are temporary and the former forever. It is suggested to place these thoughts into your hands and look at it like a child would examine a butterfly in his hands. Be aware that, during meditation, the thoughts can be any kind of thought, negative or positive as well as a memory or an abstract idea. If you're capable of directing your mind to not be reactive to every event, then the purpose of the practice has been accomplished.

Conditioning

In contrast to meditation, where you separate yourself from your thoughts, which is much more difficult to attain, however, it is more effective over the long term Conditioning alters the emotional state associated with thoughts. The process is very similar to the approach of learning for managing emotions. The main difference between conditioning and learning is that you will not simply stop at changing your perception and you'll adopt this new perspective as your default.

If a memory like this one, is associated with negative emotions, such as an unhappily split You want to train your mind to believe that when it comes back, instead of feeling sad it is a time to feel happy. The process of reorienting your perception is not permanent to this process, but the goal is to ensure it is permanent. This can be achieved with the help of meditation. You can do this by being objective and think about all the good that the tragic event resulted in.

After the breakup and re-orienting your thoughts by imagining that you wouldn't have suffered that much harm had you not equally loved and been loved by that many. Because of that you begin to think about it and realize that you're human beings capable of being loved and loving as many times as you like and that's enough for you to be happy. Every time the break-up comes back however difficult you find it, you recall the realization until it is permanent.

Of course conditioning is more complex and challenging than that, so it's important to be patient as it takes time.

It is possible to do both simultaneously to benefit from every benefit. Additionally, certain thoughts are more easily managed through meditation, while others require a lot of conditioning.

Chapter 18: Trying to Embrace Criticism

What is the best way to make critics feel better about your self-esteem? In reality, it could if you allow it. When you're criticized, you're getting an opportunity to make improvements to your behavior which is fine and absolutely nothing to be wrong about that. Do this today. When someone criticizes you, say thank you for their comments and smile to show you are thankful to have learned their perspective of things . This helps you look at things from different angles.

If you view criticism as a personal attack If you take criticism personally, you're not emotionally competent. In fact, you're likely to hold feelings of anger and blame the person who provided you with the information that can help you in your life. It isn't always a good idea to take advice. If it's completely unjustified and lacks base, you are able to accept it because the advice offered by others , there is an assessment of the current thing you're doing. This advice isn't often given when all is well. Therefore, even if you may not be a fan of the suggestion or criticism that someone or someone else has come up with but you're empathetic enough to understand that they took the time to assist in a situation that isn't satisfactory. That is, be more than the person you disagree with and appreciate their contribution. It's not all about you.

In the modern world we live in, we hear people constantly complaining about how their action was ridiculed. If you go through the personal pages of individuals on Facebook you will see many criticisms posted in the comments. Maybe a woman wants to learn how to improve her appearance or a man needs to find out how to speed up his running. In the plethora of responses the public has opinions Some of them may be legitimate opinions, whereas others are just in order to get their voices heard by the crowd. It is your responsibility to differentiate between two forms of criticism.

If you feel empathy for people whose opinions don't aid, you should acknowledge that they attempted to assist, even though it was not successful. If you look through all the answers to the question there's an ounce of hope within the answers. Maybe the girl we mentioned was not confident and was looking for positive things. Perhaps this helped her feel more comfortable with herself and appreciate what she's made of. The truth is, it does not matter what that someone has said. It's only the quality of their effort to give it a shot and frequently, you can discover answers to your life's questions by looking through the words of what people have to say.

"I believe you should make it smaller."

"I believe you should examine the balance a little."

"I believe that you are making use of the incorrect materials."

"I think that if you cut the nose smaller the nose will stay in the air for longer."

These are critiques of the current model plane , which the Facebook user tried to improve. The suggestions are useful and emotional intelligent people will not consider criticism to be any other way than beneficial. They will be grateful to those who provided feedback that they received and utilize it to improve the quality of what it was they were requesting.

Do not take the criticism personally. If someone is critical of something you are doing, simply consider:

• Is this criticism justifiable?

* What can I take away from this?

Allen was a nuisance to other people's lives all the often. When he was criticised and criticized, he took it personal and then one of his colleagues was very angry with him over the criticism he received, even though the criticism was well-intentioned.

When Allen and his friend posed the questions above, Allen found that yes the criticism was justifiable and he did possess a talent for intervening. Allen had never thought of this before. Allen had interpreted it as being involved, but his friend had advised him that engaging even when nobody wants your involvement can be seen as interference. His friend then asked him what he could take away from this experience Allen's first response was to stay clear of interfering. Since that time although he did have the habit of doing so to do so, he made a conscious effort to not give an opinion , unless requested to do so. The thing he found amusing was that, the times he didn't intervene with people, they actually asked to hear his thoughts and wanted it more than they did before. He gained more friends by practicing emotional intelligence. He smiles when he thinks about the first situation that led him to be a more empathetic person to those who surround him, and to be more understanding, rather than critical.

You've probably met a lot of people who are irritated when they are subjected to criticism. People who place themselves above criticism they've received, but in reality, no one is in any way above criticism. When you elevate yourself over it, you're declaring, "I am not emotionally capable of addressing what you're declaring." The writer who is writing a book will be ineffective without criticism. They are learning to master the art of presenting the reader with pictures using words. If the reader isn't able to recognize the image, he is foolish to write in the same way. But, if he had listened to critiques and honed the way he describes the way in which readers were drawn to his writing, he'd use the power of emotion to boost himself and his image.

Humans are meant to thrive in the face of criticism. Are you wondering why children with the same parents experience different experiences in their childhood and their surroundings, even though the individuals and places were similar? The reason is that the perception is distinct. A child might have perceived his father as uncaring. Another child might have seen his father as caring. If you can transform criticism into constructive changes and open your heart to emotional intelligence in the most effective way.

Chapter 19: Looking at Things Through A Detached Eye

Let's consider an example from a the game of baseball. If a player is connected to the game , his thoughts and emotions are influenced by the pace at which the game is taking place. If the team that he believes in is losing, he'll be able to feel that his heart is sinking. If the game is going well it will be feelings of joy. We realize that the pace of play is not under our hands, but we let ourselves be influenced to extreme levels.

It's not that you shouldn't take a break to watch a sporting event or just enjoy it. But , it is best to watch it with a neutral perspective. Do not let your emotions run through the highs and lows. The reason is that allowing external influences to regulate our emotions:

is not healthy for your mind or its stability.

It's not great for physical health either.

Effect of emotions on judgment

We all know that becoming a physician,, you require years of training studying, research, and intense research. Additionally, to all of this you require mental stability, too. Imagine a doctor caring for a person injured in an accident that is severely injured. The doctor is able to give proper treatment to the patient but only if they are separated from each other and feels calm and secure.

Operating on someone within an ICU requires complete and total concentration. When it comes to ICU, an emotion or two can result in a lack of concentration and possibly a mistake from the surgeon performing the operation. When the patient is operating even the tiniest errors can have devastating outcomes. A physician can only operate on a patient whom he's not emotionally connected.

However, if the person who is the victim of that incident occurs to be someone close to that doctor , someone in his family, one he's extremely close to, he won't be able to treat the individual. All his experience and abilities, and all the things he has learned throughout his professional career will be ineffective when he observes someone close to him hurt.

Whyis that? Simply because there are numerous emotions associated with this person. The doctor will feel the strongest of feelings like extreme stress and shock to the brain. Do you think someone who is in this mental state can be operated on by a doctor?

He might be the most skilled surgeon in the nation however, if the patient he cares about is found to be him injured, he'll become a mere victim. The surgeon is not allowed to perform surgery on his child or daughter, or any other person close to them. This is an extremely concrete illustration of how emotions can be destructive on every aspect of our existence. While this is an extreme way to show how emotions can affect our judgment however, this is exactly what we encounter everyday in small circumstances countless times.

The primary focus is to be Emotionally Intelligent

We must recognize that it is I that is the one who creates all kinds thought patterns, but it's me that allows me to be affected by the circumstances that surround me. Let's look at a movie as an example: We are aware that a film is pure fiction and that nothing occurring in it is actual. The purpose of a movie is purely entertainment purposes.

We are quite easily affected by scenes that are in it. So, if the scene isn't generating these emotions, they are permitting your mind to experience it. We are prone to be enmeshed to the characters to the point that if the characters move we also move. In the event that they cry we cry. It's the same with everyday daily life - people around us - and also the circumstances surrounding.

Also, you must be aware that it is you have complete control, total and complete control over the way you want to experience.

Do you feel at ease when being down? Do you enjoy the idea about losing temper with other people? Is this your natural instinct? If the feeling of anger, frustration, hurt and agitation can make the feeling of being calm, peaceful, and steady You can feel it. If it doesn't work, let your thoughts go now! Find how you feel peaceful and stable. It's normal.

The whole process may seem complicated at first , but trust me when I say that it's only a thought away. Just a few thoughts away from becoming an emotionally smart. All you require is knowledge and constant attention. When that awareness is firmly seated within your head, everything becomes feasible.

Through gaining control over the kinds of thoughts you would like to create and feeling how natural and powerful to you,

you are able to create your own path to success.

How can I strengthen that Belief?

We can reinforce that belief by eliminating another system of belief that we've lived our whole life. We've spent our entire life believing that the environment and other people are the ones that control our emotions. But they aren't! If you are watching a film without a solitary eye it won't trigger the emotions of a storm in the most romantic portions of the film.

Unfortunately, we've lived with this idea for many years that we've lost the ability to control our emotions. us to control our emotions. However, with a effort and a constant reminder that my thoughts aren't generated by anyone else but my own mind, I have the ability to regain control.

Are you content with what You Feel?

What are the most intense emotions people feel the most during the day? If you had to answer this question, it would be emotions that are triggered by anger or agitation anxiety, stress and, most of all, irritation.

Now , you must think about and honestly ask yourself whether you're confident in your feelings? Are you at ease when you are angered? Not at all! I'm not comfortable when I'm angry, and neither do I feel great afterward.

Most people tend to argue that anger is needed. However, it's not about justifying why anger is necessary. It is about whether it's acceptable or not! Simply put! The majority of us would say that anger isn't healthy. Not for your mind, nor for the body.

If you're not at ease with the feelings of anger, agitation or impulsiveness, anger anguish, anger, and hatred and fear, you must get yourself off the hook. Find out what you're feeling and why you feel it and then alter your emotions immediately. Now, even! Take note of that. Are you at ease and at ease? If not, then think about what you can do to make a change? Yes, definitely.

It is possible that you won't be successful immediately, but after some practice , in the course of a few times you'll see improvement and you will master each thought and emotion that you generate.

If you are able to successfully monitor and control your emotions during one circumstance, you will be able to perform it a number of times. This is the most important thing to keep in mind. All you need is regular training and monitoring.

What happens when a lack of EQ Causes Depression

It was mentioned earlier that anything we experience continuously for a long period is a habit. The mind and body become familiar with feeling anxiety, anger, frustration and all the negative emotions that we have been having for a long period of. So, if there's no solution to achieve that feeling then the person is likely to be in a state of depression. They begin to feel depressed and empty even though all the things he requires to live a happy life.

It is possible to feel as if there's something missing or there's a gap that must be filled, because his body isn't capable of producing those chemical. The person experiences depressed. That's how the process begins. The longer you stay in depression, your quality of life will continue to slide downwards and down until it reaches an extent where regaining from it is a challenge.

Why did this begin? It began when we did not check our feelings at the initial stage, and let our mind to be influenced constantly by everything that was going on. Through time we became accustomed to the fact that feeling down is normal, however it's not. Anything that does not make you feel at ease can't be normal. Do not worry, because it's not overdue. When you make an effort to determine what you're thinking, you can stop the clock.

Conclusion

I hope that this book was useful in helping you discover what makes people who are emotionally intelligent distinct.

It is the next stage to replicate these habits, and then make them your own.

Thank you for your kind words and best wishes!

www.ingramcontent.com/pod-product-compliance
Lightning Source LLC
Chambersburg PA
CBHW071837080526
44589CB00012B/1023